Sus:
Station

C000155406

David Bathurst

Photographs by David Bathurst

S B Publications

BY THE SAME AUTHOR

The Selsey Tram
Six Of The Best!
The Jennings Companion
Financial Penalties
Around Chichester In Old Photographs
Here's A Pretty Mess!
Magisterial Lore
The Beaten Track (republished as The Big Walks Of Great Britain and subsequently Best Walks
Of The North and Best Walks Of The South)
Poetic Justice
Walking The Coastline Of Sussex
Best Sussex Walks
Let's Take It From The Top
Walking The Disused Railways Of Sussex (republished as Walking The Disused Railways Of
Sussex And Surrey)
Once More From The Top
Sussex Top Tens
Walking The Kent Coast From End To End
Walking The Riversides Of Sussex
Walking The South Coast Of England
Anyone For Tenors?
Walking The Triangulation Points Of Sussex
Walking The Disused Railways Of Kent
Walking The Sussex Border Path
Walking The County High Points Of England

To Graeme and Vicky

First published in 2013 by S B Publications
Tel: 01323 893498
Email: *sbpublications@tiscali.co.uk*
Website: *www.sbpublications.co.uk*

Text and photos © Copyright David Bathurst 2013

ISBN 978-185770-3696

Front cover/title page: *Doleham Station* (p152) Front inserts: *Boxgrove Priory* (p23) &
Lindfield (p86) Back (c/w): *Blackcap* (p117), *Ifield* (p92), *Bodiam* (p129), *Rye* (p131)

Contents

About The Author

David Bathurst was born in 1959 and has enjoyed walking throughout his adult life. He moved to Sussex in 1988 and from then until the end of 2012 he worked as a legal adviser to the magistrates in Chichester and subsequently in Worthing. He has written numerous books on walking in Sussex and long-distance walking in Great Britain as a whole. When not working or walking he enjoys singing, cycling and unusual fund-raising ventures. In 2004 and again in 2007 he recited the entire works of Gilbert & Sullivan from memory and in 1998 he recited all four Gospels from memory in a single day. He has appeared on the TV quizzes *The Weakest Link* and *Eggheads*. David lives near Chichester with his wife Susan and daughter Jennifer.

Author Acknowledgements

I would like to thank Lindsay Woods of SB Publications for her confidence in me; Andy Thomas (Vital Signs Publishing) for the layout and typesetting; my ex work colleagues Graeme Miller and Vicky Brindley, to whom this book is dedicated, for their encouragement and support; and, as always, Susan and Jennifer for their love and understanding. Jennifer has been a wonderful walking companion for many of the expeditions!

Introduction

The aim of this book is, simply, to list all the stations in Sussex on the railway network – note that stations on preserved lines aren't included – and provide a described walk beginning at each one (84 in all!), and ending back at that station or at another station on the network, each designed for completion within a day or less.

I've written this book for the simple reason that many people wanting to explore the best parts of Sussex on foot won't have access to a car, and for them it may be most frustrating to read of, and want to do, a particularly good walk, only to find that accessing it requires a car journey. Even if you do have a car available, driving before or after a walk may well not be ideal; if it's been a long walk, it may not be advisable for a weary driver to be at the wheel, and unless two cars are available, linear walks will pose logistical difficulties. If you've spent all week commuting by car to work or education, the last thing you may want is more driving to access leisure activity. There is the possibility of taxis, which are expensive, or bus travel, but sadly many bus services are infrequent and often non-existent on a Sunday, which may be the only day of the week that some walkers can regularly get out into the countryside. Rail services are well publicised, easily identified and on virtually all routes in Sussex are available seven days a week. Moreover, the majority of people in Sussex live within easy reach of the rail network. The walks listed will therefore be easy to access and plan, especially when supplemented with the information provided in this book.

Though Sussex doesn't have the multiplicity of railway lines it once did, its station-based walks will still allow you to find out an enormous amount about its history, geography, beauty and variety. Set out from any of the 84 railway stations in Sussex for a day's walking and you may find yourself on the streets of a beautiful historic town or picture postcard village, wandering round an old castle or abbey ruin, striding onto a downland ridge and enjoying stunning views to the Weald, marching along a promenade watching an incoming tide crashing against the seashore, ambling along a riverbank with the enticing prospect of a pub lunch at a riverside table, or following a disused railway which puts you in touch with a fascinating aspect of our transport heritage. Even the most unpromising surroundings for a station can still produce a very good walk; one example is Gatwick Airport, from where it is only a short walk to the delightful church of Burstow and its associations with one of England's most famous astronomers.

You may be surprised to read of the scenic and/or historic beauty close to even the most bland suburban station!

Some of the walks are circular, starting and ending at the base station for that walk. However, some are linear, ending at a different station from the base for that walk, not always on the same line as the base station. So check the station map and the relevant timetable to plan your journey home. To reiterate, the stations will all be on the actual rail network and won't form part of "preserved" railways such as the Bluebell Railway; these don't necessarily link into the network and will generally require road transport to access, contrary to the ethos of this book. Also excluded are stations on novelty/fun trains such as the Dotto at Eastbourne or Volk's Electric Railway at Brighton, and termini of freight-only lines such as Ardingly.

A word of advice about travelling most economically by train. Try to travel at weekends or Bank Holidays or after 9am on ordinary weekdays if you can; travelling during the morning peak is invariably much more expensive. If you're not entitled to a discount card, e.g. by virtue of being a student or senior citizen, buy a Network card which is available to anyone, regardless of age or status, and will give you a third off standard rail fares for journeys within Sussex (on weekdays it can only be used after 10am and discounts won't apply to cheaper fares). Please note that improvement works sometimes do take place at weekends meaning that some trains are replaced by buses, but these are very well publicised in advance at stations and on the Internet.

Each walk does not pretend to take in absolutely every item of arguable architectural, cultural or scenic merit within its radius. To attempt to do this would, especially in the case of town walks, result in many excursions that would simply take too long or require more detail than a book of this nature permits. However, the aim is to ensure that you get to see the obvious architectural or scenic highlights within the radius of the walking area covered under each station, capturing the special character and nature of the surroundings.

Routes have been chosen carefully to keep to public rights of way, permissive paths, designated access land and other land e.g. common land, churchyards and parks dedicated to public use or where common-sense and popular usage indicates access will pose no difficulty. There should therefore be no risk of trespass. There is of course a difference between a short detour onto an uncultivated field for a better view and wandering into a private garden or driveway. If in doubt seek express permission of the owners. Technically access to permissive routes could be withdrawn but in my experience this is unlikely and alternative routes should be advertised in the event of such a withdrawal.

I trust that the descriptions are clear enough not to require maps but you may wish to have the relevant Ordnance Survey (OS) map with you to put each walk into context and identify surrounding landmarks. Please note that even the most up-to-date OS maps are prone to contain out-of-date information on rights of way; I am aware of a number of paths which have been significantly re-routed and which differ in their course from the mapped rights of way. Always follow the signage on the ground.

The walks are arranged alphabetically; each subheading gives the line code (see maps on pages 8-11), followed by the mileage, before a denotation of whether the walk is circular or follows a linear route to another station. The effort required for each walk is then given: *Easy* walks are designed to appeal to families, those with limited time or those who fancy a leisurely stroll, with no special equipment or supplies needed. *Moderate* walks will be more demanding and generally longer and/or will cover rougher terrain, but will be easily achievable by the average walker within a day or less. *Strenuous* walks should only be attempted in a day by fit and well-equipped walkers with proper walking shoes or boots, and shouldn't be attempted in bad weather.

The walk description itself will make it clear where supplies or refreshments may be available (so read the description before setting out) but things do change so check ahead and always have some supplies with you just in case.

Happy walking.

David Bathurst
April 2013

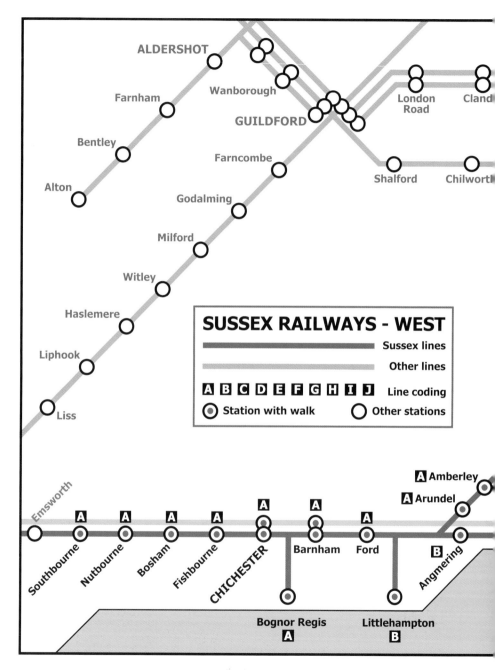

SUSSEX RAILWAYS - WEST

ALDERSHOT

Farnham

Wanborough

Bentley

GUILDFORD

Farncombe

London Road

Cland

Alton

Godalming

Shalford

Chilwort

Milford

Witley

Haslemere

Liphook

Liss

SUSSEX RAILWAYS - WEST

Sussex lines

Other lines

A B C D E F G H I J Line coding

Station with walk   Other stations

A Amberley

A Arundel

Emsworth

A Southbourne

A Nutbourne

A Bosham

A Fishbourne

CHICHESTER

Barnham

A Ford

A

B

Angmering

Bognor Regis
A

Littlehampton
B

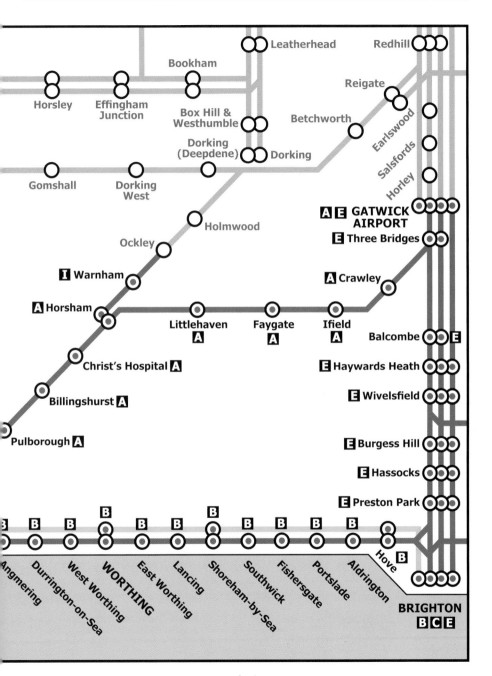

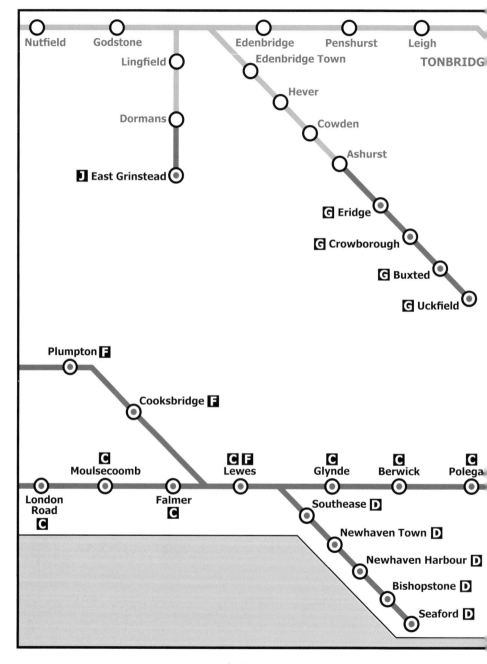

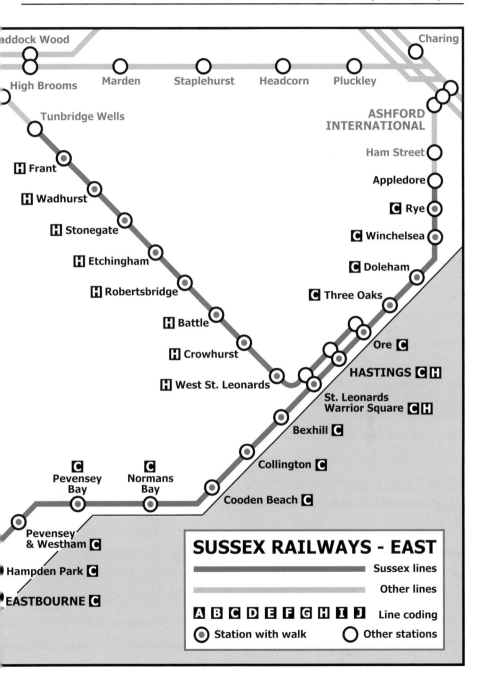

SUSSEX RAILWAYS - EAST

Sussex lines
Other lines
A B C D E F G H I J Line coding
Station with walk   Other stations

The Walks

Aldrington *(Line B, 9 miles, linear walk to Hassocks: strenuous)*

Take the north station exit and proceed down the path, turning right at the junction at the end then almost immediately left into Amherst Crescent, following it up to the A270 Old Shoreham Road; turn left, then cross over and turn right into Holmes Avenue. Walk up Holmes Avenue, passing Bishop Hannington Church and crossing over Nevill Avenue, continuing to the fine 1820 West Blatchington windmill. Beyond it bear left to cross the A2038 Hangleton Road, going straight over into Clarke Avenue and then first right, passing Poynings Drive and then veering left along Downland Drive. At the very top end bear briefly right then left as signed along the Monarch's Way footpath, heading north-westwards past a school and veering left. The views from here are sensational, including the Isle of Wight on a clear day. You pass a large green and immediately beyond it a path goes off to the left.

Here you could carry straight on down to a path junction by a bridge over the A27, turning right to join the Dyke Railway Walk and cross the bridge. Alternatively, you could take in a delightful church and the bottom end of the Dyke Railway Walk, as follows. Turn left down the path, crossing straight over at the end into Hangleton Way and following it downhill past the Downsman pub and a small parade of shops to reach the very pretty flint-built St Helen's Church with an 11th century nave and 13th century tower. Then retrace your steps past the shops, and opposite Poplar Avenue turn left up the signed Dyke Railway Walk to cross the bridge over the A27.

From here continue along the path, the course of a railway line which once linked Brighton with Devil's Dyke. This is now quite delightful walking, with superb views out to sea. The path swings north-westwards from the A27 crossing, but then swings east of north. Having passed the northern end of West Hove golf course to your left, you now become aware of another course to your right, and the clubhouse comes into view. Here the path swings more decisively right, and just beyond this bend you turn left up a narrow but clear path heading just west of north to reach Devil's Dyke Road. Cross the road and go forward to a path running parallel with it, turning left to follow it, passing through a car park and continuing gently uphill, enjoying excellent views towards the coast.

Go straight over at the next road junction and continue parallel with the road, veering right. Shortly beyond this right bend you reach and cross the South Downs

Way (SDW); shortly beyond this crossing you'll arrive at the Devil's Dyke Hotel, now an immensely popular pub and restaurant. You're now right on the edge of the South Downs escarpment and can enjoy fantastic views to the Weald, a topograph situated close by helping you to identify the places you can see from here on a clear day. Retrace your steps to the SDW, and now turn left to follow it along a clear path going gently downhill north-eastwards, keeping the spectacular Devil's Dyke ravine to your left. Legend has it that the cleft was created by the Devil who swore he'd drown the churches of the Weald by cutting through the Downs thus letting in the sea, but he was frightened off and left the job half done! At length you get within sight of a parking area and a road coming in from your right. Here you veer left, downhill, to arrive at a road at the hamlet of Saddlescombe.

Turn left onto the road then very shortly right as SDW-signed onto the farm lane, then follow the signed SDW round the farm, soon returning to the lane. Immediately beyond the buildings you reach a gate across the lane, and just beyond that, you reach forking paths going left. Take the right fork of these to join a clear path (ignore another right-forking track very shortly beyond the first fork) and head north-eastwards up onto Newtimber Hill. As you rise the main path veers away left but you carry straight on along a fainter path. You reach a field boundary with a pond to your right, going forward as signed into the field beyond. Initially the path is a little unclear but take as your line the summit of the very prominent Wolstonbury Hill ahead. Keep that directly in front of you, then as an area of trees comes in from the right, you'll see the path becoming much clearer, veering half-right from just east of north to proceed in a more north-easterly direction, dropping steeply downhill. The views are magnificent, particularly to the Jack & Jill windmills and the village and church of Pyecombe.

As you approach the hill bottom, look out for a field boundary and enclosed path coming in from the left, and arrive at a number of gates. Make sure you move to the left side of the field boundary immediately beyond the gates and follow the now clear path downhill to reach a

Looking down into the Devil's Dyke

footbridge over the A23. Cross the bridge and go straight ahead along the lane which veers north-westwards and becomes a rough and very muddy track. Go forward to a path junction beside a quarry which is to the left, bear hard right here onto a bridleway that heads uphill, south-eastwards, then having reached the top of the rise look out for and cross a stile in the fence on the left. Follow the path just west of north from the stile to reach the triangulation (trig) point atop Wolstonbury Hill, from which there are superb views in all directions most notably to the South Downs escarpment and the windmills.

From the trig point, take an obvious green path heading steeply downhill eastwards (take as your line a straight road running eastwards a little way downhill and to the left of Jill, the lower windmill). Follow it as far as the edge of trees, reaching a path junction with a bridleway sign pointing right. Turn left here, soon being reassured by a footpath sign, and continue straight on downhill along an obvious wide path heading northwards, emerging from trees and passing a house and its gardens. You reach a road onto which you turn right, following it to the A273. Immediately before the road junction look out on your right for a fine view of the extraordinary 1840 brick baronial entrance to Clayton railway tunnel. Now turn left, soon passing the welcome Jack & Jill pub, then follow beside the A273 downhill – thankfully there is a pavement – and near the foot of the hill, pass a garden centre that includes the South Downs Heritage Centre which is well worth visiting; it displays a wide range of fascinating exhibits including a blacksmith, wheelwright, vintage ploughs and other rural antiquities. Continue to a road junction with the B2116, turning right as signed towards Hassocks. The station is shortly signposted to your left.

Amberley *(Line A, 5 miles, circular walk: moderate)*

Proceed from the station down to the B2139, turning left and walking under the bridge. Shortly turn left along the road signed North Stoke, and follow the road for just over half a mile. At the T-junction at the end turn right and walk down to the church of St Mary, quite unrestored, with a Norman nave and Early English transepts. Walk back to the T-junction but this time carry on along the road uphill, following it on for just over a mile. In parts it's more of a track than a road, there's no through traffic and the views improve with every step, particularly back to the Arun valley and Arundel Park.

The road bends right and peters out at a gate, with forking tracks beyond. Take the left fork and follow the path north-eastwards, the views continuing to improve – watch out for Arundel Castle in the middle distance, and Littlehampton and the coast beyond – then beyond a crossroads path junction veer just south of east to reach an (unsigned) path T-junction. Turn left here and follow the path gently uphill north-eastwards, the gradient only steepening in the vicinity of another crossroads of paths which you go straight over, soon arriving at a junction with the South Downs Way (SDW) on top of the

The ruins of Amberley Castle

escarpment. Turn left to follow the SDW as signed westwards, climbing onto Rackham Hill. The views northwards are fantastic, particularly to the meandering river Arun and Pulborough. Carry on past the trig point, now enjoying views to the Downs escarpment ahead, including Bignor Hill, and southwards towards Arundel Castle, Bognor Regis and the sea. Sticking to the SDW, you now descend very steeply then as the ground levels out, just before Downs Farm, continue in the same direction along a narrower path which descends through trees to arrive at a road.

Turn right, soon passing (but ignoring) a road going off to the left, and carrying straight on downhill along Mill Lane to reach the B2139. Cross straight over and walk along School Road past a tea room into the centre of the very pretty village of Amberley. Pass the left turn into Church Street and, on the right, the village shop and Black Horse pub (sadly closed at the time of writing). Turn left at the T-junction by the pub and follow the road, which then veers left to a T-junction with Church Street. Your way is right, towards the parish church, but it's worth detouring back along Church Street to School Road first, as the street has so many beautiful houses. Now proceed churchwards along Church Street past the village pottery, sensational Amberley House and Norman church, and then, as the road peters out by a green and pond, continue along a footpath keeping the walls of Amberley Castle to your left. The castle was a square-towered construction dating back to the 1370s to defend the upper reaches of the Arun valley. Stay on the clear path over the railway, then continue as signposted, generally westward, across the fields, keeping straight on, soon being reassured by a footpath sign pointing ahead. Beyond a gate, look ahead for and walk to a clear footpath signpost on the embankment, pausing to enjoy the views across the river to Bury, with its 12th century church and attractive

houses including the sometime home of author John Galsworthy.
Turn left now to follow parallel with, and within sight of, the Arun, in due course reaching an impressive SDW footbridge over the river. Cross the bridge, and turn left to continue along the right river bank as far as the very photogenic Houghton Bridge. On reaching the road, turn left to follow it, passing (or visiting) the tea gardens on the far side of the Arun; just over the road here is the turning to North Stoke with the Bridge Inn just to the left if you fancy something stronger! Go forward under the railway bridge then turning immediately right for the station. Just across the station approach road is the entrance to Amberley Museum, with its displays and exhibits devoted to our industrial and transport heritage.

Angmering *(Line B, 5 miles, linear walk to Goring-by-Sea: moderate)*

From the station exit, turn left and walk down B2140 Station Road. Immediately before the church of St Mary, East Preston, just prior to the sharp right bend, turn left onto a signed footpath. However you should visit the church if it's open; it boasts a remarkably thin tower that was added around 1500, its internal width no more than six feet. The stone spire is one of only very few in the county, the north doorway of the church, of Caen stone and oak, dates back to 1130, the nave of the church dates back to the 12th century, and there is a 13th century chancel.

The pretty church at Ferring

Now follow the signed footpath referred to above, continuing past a park which is on the left. When the path ends (with a particularly attractive thatched cottage to the left) turn right onto The Street and follow it. Go over a crossroads and continue, bending left; shortly after the left bend you turn right onto Sea Lane and follow it for half a mile or so, veering left and then right and continuing in a straight line, going forward along a concrete path to arrive at the shingle beach. Turn left to follow the shingle. This is the toughest part of the walk, although at low tide you could follow the sands.

Beyond the boatyard you're able to pick up a greensward, a long strip of green providing easy walking, with the houses of West Kingston and Kingston Gorse to your left. If the tide is out you've again the option of the magnificent sands punctuated by rocks, pools and channels; there is a small collection of black rocks, visible half a mile offshore at low tide, that are believed to contain the remains of Kingston Chapel which was submerged by the sea in the 17th century. If you stick to the greensward you'll reach two gates in close succession and continue along the greensward beyond, then go forward to more shingle. However it's not quite as difficult walking as the previous shingle tramp, and in any case you have a café immediately beside you to your left. Continue past some beach huts to arrive at the paved Pattersons Walk, which you follow; for a short part of it there's the option of a raised promenade to the right, passing a pillbox. Immediately beyond an imposing cream-painted house to the left, you arrive at a very wide area of green known as Goring Gap and a small car park at what is the bottom end of Sea Lane in Ferring.

Turn left to pass through the car park, cross the road and follow a metalled path going parallel with and to the right of Sea Lane, just west of north, passing some particularly attractive cottages on the far side. Go on to cross Midhurst Drive, very shortly reaching, on the other side of Sea Lane, a gate with signs for Ferring Cricket Club and Little Twitten. Immediately to the right of the gate is a signed footpath, and you turn left across Sea Lane to follow this footpath beside the cricket pitch, soon arriving at the east end of Church Lane, onto which you turn left, passing the flint-built Maytree Cottage and Holly Cottage, and the yellow-washed Church Cottage. The street is however dominated by St Andrew's Church which dates back to 1250 with an interior full of tablets to the Henty and Olliver families. Retrace your steps down Church Lane and turn left along Ferring Street, soon arriving at a parade of shops. Go forward to cross the railway and immediately beyond the crossing turn right along a footpath (although you may be tempted by the pub just beyond!) The footpath proceeds alongside the railway line, and there are fine views all along here to Highdown Hill. Eventually you arrive at Goring Street, and can access Goring-by-Sea station immediately the other side.

Arundel *(Line A, 7 miles, circular walk: moderate – can be shortened to 1.5 miles for a town walk only)*

From the station, walk down the station approach road, turning left to walk beside the A27 and soon crossing the road using the pedestrian crossing provided. Continue beside the A27, passing the roundabout which is to the left, and go straight on along the road leading into the centre of Arundel, passing the Lido and crossing over the Arun to arrive at a mini-roundabout. The town developed as a result of its situation at the river crossing, and at one time it was a port, handling such goods as wine from France and coal from Newcastle. With the bridge immediately behind you, make your way along the street straight ahead, keeping the post office to your right and the Moat House café to your left, and walk up the hill, keeping the castle to your right and war memorial to your left. You pass a line of superb 18th century red-brick houses, including the five-bayed three-storeyed Norfolk Arms Hotel and Spencer Swaffer Antiques, all in the shadow of the castle. Although it looks ancient, the castle (the public entrance to which is off Mill Road) was in fact rebuilt in the 18th century; all that remains of its original fortification is the 12th century shell keep and fragments of the 13th century barbican and shell wall.

Cross the road and bear left along Maltravers Street to view the Town Hall to your left, then continue along Maltravers Street with its gracious red brick town houses, gradually descending. Near the roundabout at the end turn right into pretty King Street and follow it uphill to reach London Road. Turn right to arrive at the Roman Catholic cathedral, built in Gothic style in the 1870s, although it was only designated a cathedral in 1965. Cross the road and walk back down towards the centre, the yellow brick Tower House opposite, soon reaching the much older parish church of St Nicholas, dating back to the 14th century, and partitioned into separate Anglican and Catholic areas. The Catholic area, viewable only through glass, is known as the Fitzalan Chapel where former Dukes of Norfolk and Earls of Arundel lie buried, and there are some most impressive canopied tombs. Now walk past the magnificent flint-built Arundel Priory, incorporating the Priory Playhouse, straight back down the hill to the bridge. (For a shorter walk, you could simply return to the station from here.)

Immediately before the bridge turn left into Mill Road, passing the ruins of Blackfriars, a Dominican friary (to your right) and the Norfolk Centre and the public entrance to the castle (to your left). Then proceed along the left side of a delightful avenue with the bowls club, putting green and children's park on the right, going forward to cross a humpback bridge, and reach Swanbourne Lake, noting the lovely waterfall to the left. Immediately beyond the lake, there's a gateway to your left (1) which you pass through, but by following the road a little further you'll reach the popular Wildfowl & Wetlands Trust, which is well worth a visit. In its 60 acres of watermeadow you can study the lifestyles of more than 1000 swans, geese and ducks including such rare species as blue ducks from New Zealand. You'll then need to retrace your steps to continue. Pass through the gateway at (1) above and enjoy a lovely walk along the right side of Swanbourne Lake on an excellent path. Having reached the far end of the lake, continue straight on through a gate (don't veer off left) and proceed uphill, now in Arundel Park, a former deer park and 1000 acres in size. At the top of the rise, a couple of hundred yards from the gate, you reach a crossroads of tracks; turn right here then almost immediately left as signed, up a very steep hillside, aiming for a stile just to the right of woodland. You're briefly on the Monarch's Way, the longest inland named path in Britain! Beyond the stile you continue clearly onwards on the path, past a pair of trees and on to a clump of trees with a stile towards the left side of the clump. Go over the stile and continue to a footpath sign at the edge of the wood immediately ahead of you. The panorama behind you is quite stunning, stretching far beyond Arundel to Bognor Regis and the sea.

Arundel's Roman Catholic cathedral

On reaching the footpath sign at the edge of the wood, turn left to follow a track skirting the wood; beyond the wood the track bends left but you proceed as signed, aiming for a stile below, your marker being the left-hand end of a line of chalk cliffs ahead of you. The views from here to the Arun valley and the South Downs beyond are superb. Drop down to the stile, cross it and continue downhill on the obvious track, arriving at a T-junction of tracks and turning right, then shortly turning left as signed and descending even more steeply, dropping down to a wall. Walk to the left of the wall then at a gateway through the wall, turn right through it, then immediately right again onto a bridletrack through the trees with the Arun below. The track soon bends sharp left then continues on an obvious course, twisting and turning (ignore a track leading off to the right up into the hills) and at length arrives within sight of the buildings of South Stoke. As you get beyond a flint wall turn right immediately to walk beside the wall and reach a metalled road, turning left to follow it. Bear left at the fork, the road becoming a track and soon passing the pretty flint church of St Leonard, a part-Norman building with a medieval tower.

The track continues to a bridge over the Arun, but just before it turn right onto a path which follows the right bank of the river for a mile. The path then veers right into trees, and emerges onto a metalled driveway which goes forward to pass the popular Black Rabbit pub. Continue briefly along the road beyond the pub but by the Coach House turn left to join another riverside path and it's now a straightforward 1.5 mile walk along the right bank of the Arun, enjoying increasingly splendid views to the buildings of Arundel as you progress. At length you arrive at the end of Mill Road in the centre of Arundel. Turn left to reach the mini-roundabout, and left again alongside Queens Road and then the A27 to return to the station.

Balcombe *(Line E, 7 miles, linear walk to Haywards Heath: moderate)*

Leave the station by the down platform exit, climbing to London Road. Go more or less straight over onto a path which brings you to Newlands, turning right and following it round to the left, going forward into Oldlands Avenue and following it to its end. Turn left at the end into Haywards Heath Road, then turn shortly right along a signed footpath heading north-eastwards downhill, heading for the trees. You reach a fork of paths and take the right-hand fork into the woods, dropping down steeply on a flight of steps and turning right into Mill Lane. You soon cross Ardingly Reservoir and then shortly turn right onto a path which descends to and follows the left bank of the reservoir. As well as providing water supply, the reservoir is used for watersports and enjoys a fine array of wildlife and plant life. Trees include English oak, silver birch, ash, alder and Scots pine, birds include the great-crested grebe and green woodpecker, and plants include the oxeye daisy and orchid.

Follow the excellent path which in due course veers left to arrive back at the road; turn right to walk over a causeway across the reservoir, then almost immediately turn right as signed, off the road onto another waterside path. You emerge from the trees and get within sight of the watersports centre, now at the bottom end of the reservoir, and follow an excellent path with the boats immediately ahead of you and an area of green descending to the left. When you reach a wooden bench (1), look to your left and you'll see a stile beyond the green, just to the left of a car park. This is where you could leave the linear route to detour to Ardingly College and chapel. To make the detour, walk across the green to reach the stile and cross it. Follow the path beyond, fractionally north of east, reaching a T-junction of paths, now on the High Weald Landscape Trail (HWLT). Turn right at the T-junction and walk past the lovely house at Great Saucelands and a pond just beyond it on the left, then immediately past the pond turn left and walk uphill to reach the magnificent redbrick Ardingly College. The college dates back to the 19th century and arguably its greatest treasure, like at Lancing College, is its chapel, completed in 1883 in 13th century style. The views on the south-west side of the chapel are particularly good, and a plaque here marks the visit of the Queen to the college in 1958.

Retrace your steps to the bench at (1) above and turn left, continuing past the bottom corner of the reservoir and the black wooden boathouse and going slightly uphill to reach a path junction. Now turn left onto the signed HWLT, heading southwards along a

An opportunity to rest and enjoy at Ardingly Reservoir

left-hand field edge. You descend then as signed, kink right then left, descending to a footbridge. As you descend, look half-right and you'll get a great view to the Ouse Valley Viaduct, a spectacular piece of engineering on the London-Brighton railway. Cross the footbridge and veer right to shortly reach another footbridge just beyond which is a path fork. Take the left fork along a path which soon reaches River's Wood and follows through it to a crossing track immediately beyond which there's a fork. You need the left fork here, and after a couple of hundred yards you're reassured by an HWLT sign – you're also on the Sussex Ouse Valley Way – and continue just east of south on an obvious path. Pass River's Farm, go over the goods railway linking Haywards Heath and Ardingly, and then continue through trees, across a field and then through more trees. It's well defined throughout, arriving at Copyhold Lane. Turn right here, noting a magnificent tile-hung cottage by the road, follow the road over the railway, and reach a T-junction with Bordehill Lane. Turn left and follow it, taking care as there's no pavement.

Soon you reach Borde Hill Gardens, noteworthy for its rose garden, azalea ring and terraced Italian garden, as well as tremendous views. There are also refreshments! Continue along the road to a fork junction, bearing left into Balcombe Road; thankfully you soon have a pavement, and it's an easy descent to the railway bridge. However just before the bridge turn right off Balcombe Road onto a cycle path/walkway which skirts the Sainsbury's car park and arrives at a road junction beside another railway bridge. Turn left under it and you'll see Haywards Heath station on your right.

Barnham *(Line A, 12 miles, circular walk: strenuous)*

Turn left out of the station exit onto Barnham's main street and exit the village centre along Barnham Road, north-westwards. As you approach a pedestrian crossing, turn left immediately beyond Holmwood, no 75, onto a narrow path. This shortly swings right to arrive at Elm Grove South. Don't join the road but bear left along a signed footpath immediately to the right of the entrance to St Philip Howard School. The path soon veers to the right, keeping the school buildings to the left, and strikes out north-westwards along the right-hand edge of open fields, keeping a stream to the right and housing beyond. The path is good at first but becomes very overgrown. It bends right and reaches a T-junction with Church Lane, onto which you turn left. You pass the splendid Manor Farm, a timber-framed farmhouse dating back to 1600, and the pretty church of St George, then continue along Church Lane past Eastergate School, soon reaching the popular Wilkes Head pub.

The road veers right just beyond the pub and passes the pub car park, immediately beyond which you turn left onto a signed concrete footpath: this soon veers sharply right and passes Westergate College, then veers left and passes a line of garages, arriving at the east end of Ivy Lane. Turn right to walk alongside Ivy Lane to the A29. Cross over and turn right, then almost at once, and just before the pedestrian crossing, turn left along a signed path. Initially this follows a driveway

The distinctive hilltop Slindon Folly

past a lovely timber-framed thatched cottage, then forks right, maintaining an essentially westerly direction. You follow a left-hand field edge and enter a small patch of woodland, crossing a plank footbridge and reaching a path junction. Go straight on along an excellent path heading westwards through fields, enjoying lovely views towards the downs. At the far end you arrive at a T-junction with Hook Lane at a delightful assembly of buildings, notably Meadow Cottage to the left and Hook Place across the road. Turn right onto Hook Lane, soon reaching a crossroads junction.

Go straight over onto a narrow lane which bends to the right just by St Mary's church at Aldingbourne, heavily restored but with some impressive Norman features. Beyond the church, the lane then veers right again along Church Road, keeping houses to the left. Just beyond the houses bear left along an unsigned metalled road, and shortly, just before Aldinge Farm, bear right onto a footpath. Follow the path in the shade of trees for about three quarters of a mile, the path becoming a metalled lane and passing a really lovely flint cottage by Oldbury Farm which is to your right. You reach a junction with East Hampnett Lane at a right-angled bend, turning left to follow the lane, bending sharply right to arrive at the very busy A27. Turn right to walk a few yards to the indicated crossing point, crossing with immense care, then follow beside the road for a few yards to the left, bearing right onto a signed footpath along a right-hand field edge. Follow the field edge round to the left, then watch carefully as the path kinks right and left to follow the left-hand edge of the adjacent field (the path rather overgrown hereabouts!) then veers to the right, keeping to the left-hand field edge but now heading northwards. There are lovely views to Halnaker Windmill and also to your immediate objective, Boxgrove Priory church. Just before getting level with the church turn left along a signed path which passes the vicarage and reaches the end of Church Lane, here turning right up to the church. Boxgrove Priory was founded in 1117 and fell victim to the Dissolution, but the church remains and it is one of the most stunning in Sussex. Of particular note is the early 16th century ceiling painting, a rococo floral pattern including Tudor roses and de la Warre heraldry, while to the right of the nave is the astonishing de la Warre chantry of 1532, a mix of Gothic and classical style, painted and gilded with depictions of birds, flowers and human figures.

Follow the path round past the church entrance and go forward under an archway to reach the church car park, with easy access through a gateway to the very impressive ruins of the Priory itself. Continue through the car park onto a driveway which brings you to The Street, with attractive almshouses immediately in front of you. Cross the road and turn right, northwards, beside The Street. (To detour to the village store turn left and follow The Street southwards). Continue north up The Street, your roadside footpath switching to the right side of the road and providing excellent views eastwards. You soon arrive at the A285 at the village of Halnaker and turn right to walk along its main street, passing the Anglesey Arms pub as well as a number of pretty flint cottages. Initially there's a pavement, but then for a couple of hundred yards you need to walk beside this busy road with care till you get to a dip, car parking area and right-hand bend at Warehead Farm. Turn left to follow the clearly signed path north-eastwards, keeping the farm buildings to your left. Your path goes uphill through trees, to reach a gate, and here you're signed away from the wider sunken path onto a narrower one to the right on slightly higher ground. Watch as the wider track to your left veers slightly left; just to the right of the track here there's a stile, and you need to leave your narrower path (1) and walk over to the stile, climbing over it and proceeding along the obvious track beyond up to Halnaker windmill, an 18th century tower mill with white cap and sails and immortalised in verse by Hilaire Belloc. The views are sensational on a clear day, stretching along a huge stretch of coast and out as far as the Isle of Wight.

Return to the narrower track at (1), turning left to continue north-eastwards along it. It goes forward to follow a right-hand field edge, keeping vegetation and fencing to the right, but the views remain splendid. Don't go forward to the far right corner of the field, but a little before this point, join a narrow path forking into the vegetation to the right. You emerge and go forward downhill along a left-hand field edge, picking up a path on the field boundary strip and continuing down to cross a stile and arrive at the A285. Turn left to follow its right-hand side briefly, but soon look out for and take a signed footpath going off to the right, through the trees. You emerge and climb quite steeply through a field, following the path signage carefully, using a gap between the growing crops. From the crest of the hill there's a lovely view ahead to Eartham, dominated by the buildings of Great Ballards School, and surrounding hills and woods. Follow the path which now heads directly towards Eartham across the field, descending to reach a footpath junction and going straight ahead, through a kissing gate and forward along a track on a left-hand field edge, downhill. Go straight on uphill on a clear path which brings you to Eartham, a lovely village of flint cottages with a very pretty church with a most impressive Norman chancel arch.

Turn left along the road, soon reaching a T-junction by the George Inn; turn right here and follow the road, soon reaching a sharp right bend. Here turn left along a clear signed track which initially descends, then rises and levels out, giving splendid views towards the coast. The main track veers sharply left; here you continue in the same direction along another track, very soon bearing sharply left as signed along a left-hand field edge. Follow the field edge round, going forward into a wood and shortly reaching a T-junction of paths, turning right onto a clear path through the woods and following it downhill. Soon take a signed footpath leading off to the left, downhill on a right-hand field edge. You arrive at a T-junction with a track in the shade of trees, turning right and then veering left. Continue along the track downhill; immediately beyond a barn to your right you reach a path junction (2) and here turn left as signed up a grassy path parallel with a wider farm track. The path kinks left and then right to resume the uphill climb, then as you get close to the hilltop, veer left with the path to arrive at Slindon Folly. Built in the early 19th century for shooting-luncheons, it is a superb viewpoint from which you can view a wide expanse of countryside as far as Chichester Cathedral. Retrace your steps to (2) and turn left to continue down the track to arrive at a road by Court Hill Farm. Turn right here but shortly join an unsigned path going off to the left, parallel with the road, climbing steeply up through woods to reach a junction with another road. Bear left here and walk past the imposing 16th century Slindon College to Slindon village itself, turning right into Church Hill and following it past the church to its junction with School Hill (3). The continuous route bears right here, but if you've the energy, it's worth turning left up School Hill and up past the former Newburgh Arms inn, round to the left along Top Road and then left back down Church Hill. The streets are dotted with lovely cottages, most of flint, with lovely views as you descend.

From (3), bear right to reach the village pump, and here go straight over, between forking roads, along a signed narrow path which goes forward to the A29. Cross straight over onto a path which veers right initially, then veers slightly left, southwards, going straight on and ignoring a path going off left. Continue south through the lovely woodland of Slindon Common, over a crossing path, and on along a narrow enclosed grassy path, protected by gates at either end, to arrive at the A27. Cross over carefully – there is a break in the central reservation fencing to facilitate this – and go straight on along a footpath heading southwards along the east edge of Potwell Copse, going forward into Copse Lane, a stony driveway past houses. Turn left at the end into West Walberton Lane and follow it to reach the charming village green and pond at Walberton. Your way is right along Barnham Lane (not hard right into Eastergate Lane) but it's worth detouring left along Walberton's delightful village street of flint and brick cottages; there's also a pretty church with a 13th century chancel. Then follow Barnham Lane for a mile south-westwards veering southwards and turning right at the T-junction at the end to arrive back in Barnham with its excellent range of amenities including pub, shops and cafes. The station is just up the road on your left.

Battle *(Line H, 2 miles, circular walk: easy)*

Turn left out of the main station exit and make your way up Station Approach, turning right into Lower Lake and left into Upper Lake at the junction with Marley Lane. Almost immediately after joining Upper Lake you reach the Norman church of St Mary The Virgin on the right; it has a fine 15th century west tower and some impressive memorials. Continue beyond the church towards the town centre, arriving very shortly on the left at the entrance to the Battle of Hastings, Abbey and Battlefield Experience. The Abbey was built by William the Conqueror on the very place where Harold fell; the gatehouse was built in 1338 and in the various arches you can see examples of Norman, Gothic and early Renaissance architecture. You can take an interactive audio tour of the Abbey as you explore the atmospheric ruins and historic battlefield.

Continue along the High Street on the left-hand side, passing the magnificent Pilgrims Rest, a half-timbered building that dates from 1420, and walk on past some splendid tile-hung and timber-framed buildings, highlights being A Taste Of Battle and the Old Pharmacy, a timber-framed building rebuilt in the early 17th century. Continue on to the Bull Hotel, an inn dating from the 17th century, built of ashlar masonry salvaged from the Abbey kitchen. This is followed closely by Friar House, timber-framed and with steeply sloping roof, dating back to 1642. Further on is another timber-framed house, the 15th century Almonry, where you'll also find the Battle Museum of Local History and lovely gardens. Cross the road and walk back down the High Street on the other side of the road, then very shortly turn left into Mount Street. There's a remarkable variety of buildings on the left-hand side including the weatherboarded Bayeux Cottage, the robust Victorian redbrick Roman Catholic church and Zion Chapel, both 19th century, and the red-brick

The great gatehouse welcoming visitors to Battle Abbey

Old Court House. Continue along the same street up Caldbec Hill, climbing steadily, then just beyond Providence Cottage bear left up a driveway, almost immediately reaching the superbly restored Kings Mead smock mill, dating back to 1810, which is to the right. Take the path veering very slightly left as you reach the mill, and you'll arrive at the Kings Mead open space, where a trig point is situated, and there's a tremendous view across the countryside to the north and west. Retrace your steps to the road and turn right, crossing over and now walking down Caldbec Hill (going forward into Mount Street) following the left-hand side. There is a magnificent trio of timber-framed cottages names

Thurkill, Lewinscroft and Alfric, and as you get near the High Street, you reach the superb 15th century King's Head, a masterpiece of tile-hanging.

Return to the High Street, turning left and proceeding past another typical Victorian chapel, dating back to the early 1880s and boasting a particularly intricate doorway. You pass an alleyway leading to Abbey Court – look up at the sign Newbery Preserves which reminds us that the Newbery Jam Factory started here in the late 19th century – and go forward to Langton House, now the Battle Memorial Halls. It began in the 16th century as a two-storeyed half-timbered building, another storey being built around 1700, a new front being added in the 18th century and shopfronts appearing in the 20th century. Continue from there on to Yesterday's World, a wonderful place for discovering the colours and flavours of yesteryear, with over 30 authentic room and shop settings housed in a 15th century Wealden hall house. Collections include Queen Victoria's personal effects and nightdress and attractions include a 1930s country railway station, a 1950s cycle shop and a Victorian fudge marquee. From here, go straight on past St Mary's Church and retrace your steps to the station.

Berwick *(Line C, 10 miles, linear walk to Eastbourne: strenuous)*

Head southwards from the station along Station Road, keeping to the right-hand side. Soon a parallel cycle path becomes available, so use that to continue, enjoying good views to the South Downs escarpment. The cycle path ends and there's then a short walk along the roadside, but take the next right turn, Pound Lane, to a crossing of the busy A27. Taking great care, cross straight over to walk up Berwick's main street, noting the Cricketers Arms to your right, and bear left opposite it to join a footpath. Very shortly you reach a pond to your right; just beyond it, bear round to the right, and follow the path, which narrows considerably and goes forward to arrive at a field, with Berwick church at the top end. Aim for the top left corner of the field, and make your way to it, then continue past the church, keeping it to your right, to pass through a small area of trees. Here you can conveniently detour to visit the church, with its stunning paintings on the pulpit and chancel wall – the work of members of the Bloomsbury Group. You emerge from the trees and now, ignoring paths going off right and left, go straight on along the path heading just west of south, heading downhill then up, dipping again before rising to meet a road. Continuing on the road in roughly the same direction, descend to arrive at Alfriston, going straight on into the village centre. Its High Street boasts a mixture of styles including tile-hanging, weatherboarding and brick and timber. The Star boasts ceiling timbers decorated with carved animals, and on the street corner beside the Star is a large red lion, the figurehead of a 17th century Dutch ship. There are ample refreshment opportunities in the village.

Walk along the main street as far as St Andrew's Church, just beyond which turn left down a narrow alleyway and, reach the edge of the green, dominated by the splendid 14th century parish church. Walk across the green, passing (or visiting) the church and going over to the far corner to visit the 14th century Clergy House, acquired by the National Trust in 1896. Then retrace your steps past the church, this time though following the green round to the right to reach the bank of the Cuckmere River, turning left to follow the bank to the footbridge. Cross it and go forward along the path to reach a road. Turn right and immediately left up a signed path which soon arrives at a field and proceeds uphill on the left-hand field edge; there's a super view across the Cuckmere meadows south of Alfriston from the top corner. Continue then into the trees along a firm path, soon reaching a signed path pointing left to medieval Lullington church, well worth a visit; it is a fragment of the original and is one of the smallest in Britain, with room for barely two dozen people. Return to the firm path and follow it to a road, turning left and walking uphill, crossing the South Downs Way (SDW) and then descending, with lovely views to the left. Just under a mile from joining the road you reach Wilmington, passing a car park and then the remains of a Benedictine priory (not open to the public)

Alfriston's Star Inn, and its watchful guard

and adjacent church before reaching the village centre with its lovely buildings of flint, brick, thatch and timber. The part-Norman church of St Mary and St Peter has a yew in the churchyard (just to the right of the church entrance) that's reputed to be 1600 years old.

Walk back out of the village the way you came into it, and pretty much opposite the car park adjacent to the priory turn left onto a signed footpath for the Long Man. Initially the path goes parallel with the road then swings south-eastwards, climbing and passing through a gate then going straight on to reach the fence protecting the Long Man, a 226ft high hill figure carved into the chalk, the origin of the figure still a mystery. At the fence you reach a T-junction of paths, turning right to contour the hillside and keeping to the upper path. At length you reach a gate, beyond which you turn left to follow a path which now rises steeply upwards, soon reaching the SDW coming in from your right. Turn left onto the SDW, following it round to the right, uphill, enjoying superb views southwards to the coast. The track bends sharp left and levels out, going forward to a gate on a firm green course. However as it levels out, you should detour shortly to the left across the rough grass to mount the tumulus on the summit of Windover Hill from which you can clearly see the sea, the port of Newhaven, the South Downs escarpment westwards to Firle Beacon, and a huge tract of East Sussex farmland looking north. Then return to the SDW and proceed to the gate (1).

Pass through it, keeping Tenantry Ground, a dramatic dry valley, to your right, and soon you reach a signed fork junction, veering left here and continuing along the SDW, soon going over a crossroads of tracks (2). Between (1) and (2) it's possible to detour to the trig point on the summit of Wilmington Hill (Note: this detour isn't along designated rights of way and it appears to be outside access land but there are no apparent restrictions on access.) To make the detour, at (1) don't veer right with the SDW but go straight on uphill, keeping the fence just to your left, and pass through a hilltop gate, continuing close to the fence on the left to reach the trig point and, a few yards further on, a hillock. From here the panorama is astonishing, now encompassing the coastline eastwards to Eastbourne, Hastings and beyond. Return to and pass through the hilltop gate and EITHER retrace your steps to (1) to pick up the continuous route as described above OR it should be possible for you to immediately turn left along a path, indistinct at first then clear, along the left-hand field edge then veering very gently away from the field edge, downhill, to arrive at the crossroads of tracks at (2) above, turning left to pick up the SDW and the continuous route again. Now, whether you've detoured or not, simply proceed along the signed SDW; this is all quite magnificent walking, the views particularly good towards the coast.

As you reach an area of woodland you need to follow the SDW signage carefully, veering left into the woods and dropping down steeply. You go over two sets of path crossroads in the woods, then drop down more gently between fields, to pass the flint-built Jevington Church which boasts a Saxon west tower and also some Norman and Early English work. It's then a straightforward descent to the road in the centre of the village, arriving more or less opposite the Hungry Monk restaurant, the birthplace of banoffee pie in 1972! By turning left you could follow the road up to the Eight Bells pub and the (private) flint-built Jevington Place but

The Bloomsbury Group's artwork in Berwick church

your way is right, soon passing the Jevington Tea Gardens and then immediately bearing left as (SDW) signed up a road which soon becomes a track.

It's quite a slog eastwards up the hill, but you're rewarded by increasingly good views and at length you veer south-eastwards to pass the trig point just to the left of the path. This is the summit of Willingdon Hill, a magnificent viewpoint which you should detour to enjoy. Then continue along the SDW, the path proceeding decisively south-eastwards on the tops of the Downs with tremendous views throughout; you pass a golf course and just under 2 miles from the triangulation point you reach the A259. Just before the road veer right with the track to reach the road, cross it and continue on the SDW along the hilltop, following the obvious path. In about a quarter of a mile, now on Warren Hill, you reach a fork of paths with a trig point between the two paths. The SDW has been re-routed along the right-hand path and it's worth detouring along it to view the trig point with its superb views to Eastbourne, Beachy Head and the sea, but to make progress you actually take the former SDW on the left-hand path. This descends quite steeply, just south of east, reaching a path coming in from the right and here veering round to the left, just north of east, and dropping down to Paradise Drive, the former start of the "inland" section of the SDW. You're now entering the suburbs of Eastbourne. Turn right into Paradise Drive, following it to a junction with Carlisle Road. Turn left to follow Carlisle Road eastwards, then in few hundred yards turn left into Meads Road, following signs for the town centre. You veer slightly right with the road and reach the very impressive Town Hall, going forward into Grove Road with shops and cafes on each side. At the end you reach a roundabout, turning right here. Eastbourne town centre is straight ahead and the station is just across the road.

Bexhill *(Line C, 5 miles, circular walk: moderate)*

Turn left out of the station exit (not hard left into Station Road) and proceed northwards up Sea Road, going forward into Upper Sea Road, following it uphill until the road bends sharply left, in Bexhill Old Town. Having admired the very impressive timber-framed building to the left on the corner, bear right into De La Warr Road; to the right are the Manor Gardens with sensational rhododendrons and lovely sea views. Cross straight over De La Warr Road opposite the entrance to the gardens into Church Street with attractive brick and weatherboarded houses, highlights including Spyers Cop, Hope Cottage and Wishing Well Cottage, and on the right No 5B Little Lychgate boasts a quite beautiful garden. The Norman church of St Peter contains a tower that dates back to 1070, but its most famous relic is the so-called Bexhill Stone, a sandstone slab of 8th century origin, thought to be the lid of a reliquary containing the bones of a saint.

Walk through the churchyard past its main (west) entrance, and beyond the church veer round to the right on the church path to reach the start of a signed footpath going off to the left (north), signed "Crowhurst 3." Bear left onto this path, almost immediately crossing over the A259 and walking between the houses, crossing over Lychgates Close and continuing along the path, more of an alleyway, to Rectory Way. Bear left along it then right along the alleyway, marked with a "no cycling" sign; it now continues just east of north, crossing Church Vale Road and Chantry Avenue and arrives at the A2036 Wrestwood Road. Turn right to follow it, enjoying lovely views to the open countryside to the left. You pass St Mary's School and in just under half a mile and more or less opposite The Glades to the right, turn left onto a signed path, part of the 1066 Country Walk. Follow a right-hand field edge to the end of the field, then continue into the next field in the same north-easterly direction, passing to the right of Upper Worsham Farm, aiming to the right of the barns. As you reach the top of the rise, note a pretty flint cottage ahead; aim just to the right of it, losing height a little, and go forward onto a public byway heading northwards, past the cottage. Rising gently you reach a footpath crossroads (1) at the south-west corner of woodland, going straight over onto the Crowhurst-signed path. You now follow a really lovely path through the woods, descending to reach a brick bridge which carried the now defunct Bexhill-Crowhurst railway. Bear right up steps to turn right onto the course of the old line, recently converted into a super footpath. In half a mile or so you meet the 1066 Country Walk again (2) with a sign for VIEWPOINT ahead, keeping straight on until the path narrows dramatically and falls away. From here there are indeed superb views both to the north and to the south-east across Filsham Reedbed Nature Reserve.

Retrace your steps to (2) above but this time turn left to follow the 1066 Country Walk past Little Worsham Farm, swinging right at the path junction and arriving

An imaginative mill conversion in Bexhill old town

back at the path crossroads at (1) above. From here retrace your steps back to Wrestwood Road but then go straight over onto another alleyway which proceeds very pleasantly between houses, crossing Portfield Close and arriving at the bottom end of Rectory Way where the alleyway ends. Walk briefly along Rectory Way then left into Lychgates Close; follow it to between nos 25 and 27 where you reach the alleyway you followed originally. Turn left up the alleyway and retrace your steps via Bexhill Old Town and Upper Sea Road to Bexhill station.

Billingshurst *(Line A, 6 miles, circular walk: moderate)*

Leave the station by the "up" platform exit and cross over the road, going straight over into Myrtle Lane onto a path which very soon veers left and then right to proceed parallel with the railway line and arrive at Natts Lane. Turn right onto this road, arriving at a T-junction. Bear left here, then take a footpath which shortly goes off to the right, very soon reaching a junction of paths; take the left fork which continues south-westwards, climbing a flight of steps and crossing the A29. Go straight on following a path on the other side, along the left-hand edge of woodland, observing the path signposts. You reach a metalled crossing road, and a choice of paths going right and left beyond the metalled road; you need to take the left-hand one which enters Great Lordings Wood. Follow the fingerposts carefully along a path which proceeds south-westwards through the wood and veers right, westwards, firstly along a lovely path along the left-hand edge of the wood, and then along the right-hand field edge with the wood immediately to your right. The woodland recedes and you continue through the field in the same westerly direction to reach a road. Turn left and immediately right along a signed path towards Tanners Farm, taking care to follow the signed path past the farm and then walk uphill along a right-hand field edge, veering south-westwards to reach an area of trees, and a gate. Beyond the gate you reach a T-junction with a farm track, turning right to follow it, soon veering left (westwards) along the left edge of a wooded hill; the surroundings are delightful, with the Arun valley now opening out before you. You have the option either of the farm track or a parallel path to the right, but you then have to return to the track, going downhill to the valley bottom.

The farm track veers right, and here you need to fork left (effectively the same direction), crossing a plank footbridge and going forward to a gate, entering a field and following a right-hand field edge. Pass through a metalled gate to your right, to arrive at the towpath of the Wey and Arun Junction Canal. The canal opened in 1816 and closed in 1871, once carrying a vast range of goods, and it's gradually being restored with some fine stretches of water and rebuilt locks and bridges. Bear left to follow it to a quite beautiful redbrick footbridge over the canal, a lovely place to linger on a warm sunny day. Retrace your steps and now continue beside the canal along the towpath, soon passing Lording's Lock and working waterwheel – a splendid feature in superb surroundings – and crossing the Arun by means of an aqueduct. Continue along what's part of the Wey South Path, north-eastwards, soon reaching the bank of the meandering Arun. Veer left to walk beside the river through woodland, then veer right, north-eastwards again, along a path crossing Guildenhurst Bridge and, with the Arun close by to your right, passing Guildenhurst Farm and reaching the A272 at Newbridge.

Cross over the A272 and continue along a path which follows the canal for about three quarters of a mile, past the Northlands Lift Bridge and then Rowner Lock to a crossing bridleway just short of pylons. Turn right onto the crossing bridleway, soon veering right to pass over the Arun with its impressive weir, then left, going uphill, and right again past the buildings of Rowner Farm to reach a road. Turn right to follow the road for roughly a quarter of a mile, then left along the lane signed for Tedfold, heading east. In just over half a mile you reach a junction; you need to fork right along a signed path which heads south-eastwards, negotiating a succession of fields and stiles, and reaches an area of trees. Go straight on here, ignoring the path going off hard right here, crossing a

A delightful section of the Wey & Arun Junction Canal

track and passing a cricket ground, going forward over the field along a clear path to the A29. A slipway brings you up to a bridge which you use to cross over the road, then turn immediately left, parallel with the A29, and fork very shortly right along a path which becomes an alleyway between houses. You soon cross over Maple Drive and go forward to Coombe Hill (no hill!), bearing right then shortly left between buildings to reach the Jengers Mead shopping area.

  It's now a short walk to Billingshurst High Street (ample refreshment) onto which you turn right, following it to the junction with the A272; at the angle between the main street and this left turn, walk up a path to the church with its massive spire and Tudor entrance porch of brick and timber. Bear left up the path beside the church, admiring the delightful brick-built Churchgate Cottage to your left, then fork round the end of the church and veer round again to its south side. Here you bear left onto a path heading southwards through the churchyard and then between houses, descending and then rising, passing a park and veering right (south-westwards) to reach Station Road. Turn left to follow the road downhill to the station which is on your left.

Bishopstone *(Line D, 3 miles, circular walk: easy - NB. NO REFRESHMENTS)*

Leave the station via the footbridge and the north exit and walk straight down Station Road, crossing firstly a minor road then the A259. Immediately beyond join a signed footpath which proceeds north-eastwards along the flat valley floor, the ground rising immediately to the right. The path follows an obvious straight course, arriving at a wall that you cross by a ladder stile, then you veer northwards along a clear path through the fields, aiming for Bishopstone church. You arrive at Bishopstone Road and you follow this northwards through the old village, noting the fine white manor house on the right, but you should detour to the left to visit the church, much of which pre-dates the Norman Conquest; the porch boasts a Saxon sundial, and under the tower there's a coffin lid decorated with 12th century carving. Returning to the road, continue through the old village, passing some splendid houses, notably Monksdown and the lovely Barrack Cottage. Now follow the road out of the old village, veering northwards with lovely views opening out to the left. In less than half a mile from old Bishopstone you arrive at Norton, the road veering to the left to pass the imposing Norton House and dipping a little to reach a crossroads of ways, a "No Through Road" warning sign ahead. Bear left, south-westwards, here, and rise steadily on a grassy track. At the top of the

the hill you can enjoy magnificent views to Newhaven, the mouth of the Ouse and Newhaven Heights behind. The track, on reaching the crest, veers to the right but you go straight on over the grass to arrive at a wire fence, and you here turn left to follow a path south-eastwards keeping the fence hard to the right, enjoying lovely views to the right, and also down to Bishopstone church to your left. The path drifts away from the fence as you reach Rookery Hill, and continues some way inland of the fence, but there's no obstruction to your detouring to the trig point, from which the views both to Newhaven and to

Bishopstone church from Rookery Hill

Seaford Head on the horizon in front of you are excellent. Keeping to the path, you now begin your descent, but soon join a path signing you over the fence and then parallel with the fence but to the right of it, dropping down to the valley floor and bearing right to arrive back at Bishopstone Road. Turn right to follow it until just before the A259 you take a narrow signed path going left. This shortly brings you to the A259 onto which you turn left, shortly crossing the road and bearing right to reach and follow Station Road back to the station.

Bognor Regis *(Line A, 3 miles, circular walk: easy)*

Take the main station exit onto Station Road and turn left to follow it, going forward down London Road, the town's main pedestrianised shopping street. At the bottom turn right into the High Street, going past the Methodist Church and reaching Waterloo Square, its pleasant gardens bordered by a number of gracious stuccoed and balconied buildings, many of which date from the 19th century.

Walk to the far side of Waterloo Square and turn left to follow a path through the park down its west side, but leave the park to turn right into Manor Place, following it past the bottom of the pretty Steyne Gardens to reach the coast road at the bottom of West Street. On its far side is the white stucco'ed Royal Norfolk

Hotel with gilded arms on the pediment; it's also worth detouring up West Street to view the town museum in the old Berkeley Arms pub (note the still extant inn sign). Whether you've detoured or not, cross the coast road just west of the end of West Street and climb onto the promenade, following it eastwards past the Royal Hotel which is to your left, soon reaching the pier. When originally built in 1865 it boasted a 1000ft jetty, the toll being 1d with 4d for bathchairs. Latterly it's been the venue for the popular annual Birdman Rally, where all sorts of weird and wonderful devices are used by competitors to fly off the end of the pier!

Now continue your walk eastwards beyond the pier along the promenade, keeping the Esplanade parallel with you to your left and enjoying the sea to your right. Watch for the impressive Regis Centre, incorporating the Alexandra Theatre, to your left, then as the road swings inland, just before the frothy white buildings of Butlins (which came to Bognor in 1960) you descend along the slipway to follow the road, actually Gloucester Road, inland to a T-junction with the High Street. Turn right onto the High Street then shortly left, across the road, to enter Hotham Park through a gateway. Hotham Park is named after Sir Richard Hotham, a wealthy Southwark hatter, who in the 1780s made it his mission to convert Bognor into an elegant seaside resort and encourage Royalty to visit. He was responsible for not only the park but the fine ten-bay Hotham House with it, built for his own occupancy, and both dating back to around 1790. Your path immediately passes just to the right of the house, with the bandstand on the lawns to the right. You reach a path junction just beyond the house, turning left to follow the sign for the boating lake, at once passing the impressive clock tower immediately adjacent to Hotham House.

Continue past the boating lake, keeping the miniature railway to your right, and a pretty conservation garden and pond to your left. Follow the path on to the far end of the park then swing right, keeping a wall immediately to your left and arriving at another signed junction, with a path heading left out of the park past toilets. Continue along the path bearing gently right, signed PLAY AREA/PUTTING/ CRAZY GOLF, and you follow this path through the trees, arriving at a "mini-roundabout" path junction. Turn left here and walk along the path which brings you to the main park entrance/exit; keeping the car park and putting green to your left, you now veer right to exit the park by a roundabout. Turn hard left here into Hotham Way and follow it north-westwards. Over the road are several fine buildings, the highlight being Dome House, built in late Palladian style around 1787 in the hope that royalty would visit the town. The house is slightly concealed from the road; look out for the University of Chichester sign, the driveway beside which leads to the house. A little further on, on the same side, is the splendid line of redbrick houses known as Spencer Terrace, built around the same time as the Dome, followed by the equally impressive Redgate House. Immediately beyond the subway, bear left and walk across to the toilet block,

The imposing Royal Norfolk at Bognor Regis

bearing right through the car parking area to arrive at London Road. Turn left to follow it past the library, arriving at a crossroads junction with Lyon Street, turning right into Lyon Street West which shortly bends left to arrive back at the station.

Bosham *(Line A, 3 miles, circular walk: easy)*

NB. Part of this walk is impassable at high tide; tide tables are available on the Internet if you want to save yourself a wait!

From the station, head southwards down Station Road (immediately adjacent to the station building) and reach a roundabout junction with the A259. Cross straight over the roundabout into Delling Lane and walk southwards along the lane to a T-junction with Bosham Lane. Go straight over onto a metalled path which heads southwards for a few hundred yards to reach The Drive; continue along The Drive in the same direction, soon turning right into Harbour Road and arriving at the embankment path by the harbourside. Turn right to follow the path, aiming for the village centre, guided by the spire of the village church. This is a lovely walk with beautiful views across the harbour. At the end by the fine Mariners café turn left and then right along Shore Road (this floods at high tide) arriving at the lovely green of Quay Meadow. Turn hard right to follow the near side towards the church and the left end of the High Street, detouring to the lovely stream and waterfall to the right; then cross the green to the far left corner before making your way over the green round to the church past the very impressive war memorial. The pre-Norman church boasts a Saxon tower and chancel arch, and there is a superb Early English east window of 1120 and a crypt that was built around the same time. Its most famous worshipper was King Harold who received communion in the church in 1064. Leave the church along the path taking you to the High Street, turning left along this street past the popular Anchor Bleu pub and pretty

17th and 18th century flint and brick cottages with such august names as Bosham Castle and Bosham Abbey! Turn left at the end into Bosham Lane, soon reaching Bosham Walk, a complex of arty/crafty shops to your left, and there's another excellent café in the complex. Continue along Bosham Lane,

The view from Quay Meadow, Bosham at high tide

following it round to the right past the popular Millstream Hotel. Turn left into Delling Lane and retrace your steps to the station.

Brighton *(Lines B, C & E, 2.5 miles, circular walk: easy)*

From the station walk straight down Queens Road, passing the very prominent and ornate Jubilee clock tower (built in 1888 to celebrate Victoria's Golden Jubilee) and continuing down towards the seafront. Go forward into West Street as far as the exceptional early Victorian church of St Paul, which is to your right, boasting a fantastic spire. Walk back up West Street but before you reach the clock tower turn left into Cranborne Street, rising and walking straight on past the huge modern Churchill Square shopping complex and continuing along Western Road. Turn left into Preston Street, soon turning left and then right into Regency Square, following it to the promenade with the ruins of the 1866 West Pier immediately in front of you; this will be the site of the planned i360 Tower. Turn left onto the promenade, going beneath the 19th century Italian Renaissance-style Grand Hotel towards Brighton Pier past the Brighton Fishing Museum into what's known as the Artists Quarter with its little shops and galleries along the promenade on the inland side. Shortly before the pier climb the steps to follow beside the coast road. You'll soon reach a cluster of attractions: Brighton Pier, also known as Palace Pier and built in 1899, the impressive Brighton Wheel, reminiscent of the London Eye, Volk's Railway, billed as the oldest electric railway in the world, built in 1883, and the Sea Life Centre, the world's oldest operating aquarium, just across the road to the left of the Wheel as you look east.

At the roundabout by the Sea Life Centre immediately above the pier, head back along the coast road (Grand Junction Road) briefly, then as it bends slightly right, turn right by the Mariner into East Street, full of excellent shops and restaurants. Follow it past a turning to Pool Valley, boasting the Mock Turtle, one of the finest traditional teashops in the country. Just before the end, turn left up Market Street, swinging left and reaching Brighton Place. Turn right here, then left into Meeting House Lane. You're now in the heart of the Lanes, a labyrinth of streets of medieval origin although the current ones date back mainly from the 19th century. Follow Meeting House Lane past the jewellery shops, bearing right at the T-junction, shortly left and right again, then immediately left into Union Street. Follow this to a T-junction with Ship Street, turning right here then shortly left into Duke Street with its splendid shops including, on the right, the legendary chocolate shop Choccywoccydoodah.

At the top of Duke Street turn right to arrive at the clock tower, turn right to follow North Street downhill, then turn left into New Road. You then bear immediately right into gardens, following signs to Brighton's finest building, John Nash's Pavilion dating between 1815 and 1822, at the far end, then head for the signed Museum and Art Gallery at the north end of the gardens. Go to the top north-eastern end of the garden and turn left into Church Street, following it westwards to the junction of New Road and Jubilee Street. Turn left into New Road to view the Dome entertainment centre which is to the left, and the redbrick pillared Theatre Royal and astonishing Unitarian Church on the right. Retrace your steps down New Road and now go straight ahead into Jubilee Street, passing the modern eco-friendly Library; at the end turn left into North Road and second right into Kensington Gardens, now in the cosmopolitan North Laine area. At the end turn right and almost immediately left into Sydney Street, then at the end right into Trafalgar Street and left into Pelham Street, going straight on via St Peter's Street into Ann Street to reach the amazing church of St Bartholomew, built to

Brighton seafront's newest attraction, The Wheel

the same dimensions as the Ark! When built in the 19th century it was the biggest brick church in Europe, magnificently decorated with oil paintings and Italian mosaics. Turn left up Ann Street, continuing up the steps (Fenchurch Walk) then at the very top turn left, going straight on to a T-junction with Trafalgar Street. Turn right here, passing the Toy & Model Museum and going under a bridge. Beyond the bridge turn hard right to find yourself back at the station.

Burgess Hill *(Line E, 3.5 miles, linear walk to Hassocks: easy)*

Turn right out of the main station exit and then immediately right again, down and through the station car park, going straight on along a path parallel with the railway line which is just to your right. A little over half a mile from the station, as you get level with a railway bridge (the first to be reached), you reach a junction of paths. Turn left here, aiming just to the right of the water tower. You walk gently downhill to cross a stream, then rise again, passing immediately to the right of the tower and going straight on along a driveway which brings you to Ockley Lane. Turn right to follow this road, then in a couple of hundred yards turn left onto a signed bridleway, initially a driveway to houses and then going straight on along a rougher track heading just east of south then just west of south through the trees. Shortly you have the opportunity to join a parallel footpath to the right, providing better views. Whichever course you take, you'll reach the lovely 18th century Oldland windmill, a post mill and octagonal brick round-house with sails in situ. You reach a T-junction of paths here, turning left to follow a byway briefly, but almost immediately bear right onto a lovely parallel path with magnificent views, heading south-eastwards but veering southwards. The path peters out so rejoin the byway, here the metalled

Tudor grandeur at Ditchling

Lodge Hill Lane which descends quite steeply and veers left. As it veers right (1) go straight on into Boddingtons Lane and follow this rougher lane to reach Ditchling High Street.

Turn right to follow High Street. On the east side of the street is Conds Cottage, sometime home of writer Esther Meynell and more recently Margaret Milnes who opened an art gallery in the cottage, and next door to Conds Cottage is the house where the sculptor Eric Gill lived for a time. A signpost points off the street to the museum, housed in the old village school, where some of Eric Gill's calligraphy designs and woodcuts have been housed, and it's certainly worth the detour. Then continue along the High Street to the crossroads in the village centre, turning right here into West Street and walking past the popular café and on to the very pretty St Margaret's Church with Norman and Early English features. Almost opposite the church over the road is the superb timber-framed Wing's Place, of Tudor origin, and immediately west of that is another fine timber-framed house Cotterlings. Beyond Cotterlings, cross over and turn right immediately west of the churchyard along a lane with the village pond and museum visible to the right, arriving at point (1) above.

Turn left here back onto Lodge Hill Lane then as the lane bends right, continue straight on westwards along a signed path across fields. Beyond a field boundary the path veers to the right, and as you follow it north-westwards, there's a super view up to Oldland windmill. You soon arrive at another field boundary but just before it turn left and head southwards close to the right-hand field edge. Go straight on at a signed junction of paths and continue just west of south, going parallel with and immediately to the right of Silverdale, reaching the B2116 Keymer Road. Turn right onto it, soon reaching the centre of Keymer, passing (or possibly visiting) the partially timber-framed Greyhound Inn which is to the left, the part-Norman church of St Cosmas and St Damian to the right, and Keymer Manor House, a four-bay aisled 14th century medieval house on the left. Now simply keep on Keymer Road, soon reaching the centre of Hassocks with its many shops and cafes. To reach the station, bear right to follow Station Approach to its end.

Buxted *(Line G, 11.5 miles, linear walk to Crowborough: strenuous)*

Walk from the station exit to the adjoining A272 and turn left to follow it briefly, then bear left into Church Road, following it past Buxted church and into Church Lane, enjoying good views to the left. The road becomes a track which peters out; carry on along the obvious path down the hillside, aiming for the edge of the woods close to the railway. Watch for the Vanguard Way (VW) signpost (you will now be sticking to the VW all the way to Ashdown Forest) and follow a very rough VW-signed path through the trees, crossing the railway and continuing along the path beyond, emerging from the trees and following the right-hand field edge uphill. Veer right and walk uphill along the edge of the woods, turning right onto Fowly Lane, then shortly bear left into a field. Follow it downhill as signed, aiming for the right-hand field corner, dropping steeply to enter more trees and follow a path, initially narrow then widening to become a lane past Holders Farm. The lane veers left and you follow it to just beyond the Hurstwood Farm turning. Continue ahead as signed, north-westwards, past Mount Pleasant Farm to reach a T-junction with a road; cross over and turn immediately left along a narrow path, parallel with the road, then veer right, downhill, along the obvious but still narrow path in the shade of trees. Emerging, you veer to the left, north-westwards, through fields and past the attractive 19th century High Hurstwood church to reach another road. Turn right to follow it briefly then as it bends right go straight on as VW signed, down past the beautifully situated Woodpeckers cottage, taking care to go just to the left of it over the bridge.

An excellent grassy path now takes you north-westwards, uphill, through a succession of fields, the views getting better all the time. Watch carefully for a signed sharp turn to the left (westwards) taking you below the buildings of Stroods which are to your right, then having descended some steps you bear sharp right to pass to the left of the buildings. Turn right just past the buildings as VW signed, crossing the approach road and walking through the trees, joining an excellent track with good views to the right. You head northwards through the woods, then emerge from them, veering right but keeping the trees immediately to the right; again you enter the trees within the path before veering left, as signed, and then right to reach the buildings of Newnham Park Farm. The path goes up to a gate, which you pass through, and you then walk past the farm buildings to reach the busy A26. Cross with care and turn left to walk beside the road briefly (to the right there's a pub) then bear right as signed. Initially a grassy track, it then strikes out across the open heath and sandy soil of Ashdown Forest. The path continues north-westwards, its course very obvious; you descend then rise steeply and continue straight on, ignoring turnings off, rising all the while and arriving at Kings Standing Clump and a junction of the B2026 Maresfield-Hartfield road and the B2188 Groombridge road. Turn right then fork immediately left onto the B2026, but then straightaway turn right onto the VW track which follows parallel with and just to the right of the B2026. You cross the Wealdway, and continue along the track, which in a couple of hundred yards negotiates a short but obvious rise. At the top you reach a crossing path.

Turn left here and follows the crossing path down to the B2026; go straight over into the Four Counties car park and walk through it, turning right at the end and going forward to an informative topograph from which there are superb views across Ashdown Forest and beyond. Return to the road and turn left to follow it for a couple of hundred yards to its junction with Kidds Hill. Cross over and walk between these two roads across a grassy area just to the right of a large clump of trees, to join a clear track which climbs, levelling out with the lovely trees of Gills Lap (Galleons Lap for Pooh fans!) to the right. Descend a little with the

Gills Lap: A.A. Milne immortalised at the top of Ashdown Forest

track, looking out carefully on the left for a path leading shortly to an A.A. Milne memorial stone. The views from here are absolutely stunning. Retrace your steps to the B2026/Kidds Hill junction and this time go straight over onto a barriered path opposite the Kidds Hill turning. Shortly a path comes in from the left and soon after that there is a path forking to the right. Join that path but almost immediately turn left onto a track which now heads south-eastwards. Just keep following it in a straight line, initially uphill with a line of trees to the right, then as it levels out it continues an obvious course, crossing the Wealdway and then a further crossing track, going forward onto a rougher juicier track which arrives at the B2188 at Deerswood Farm. Go straight over onto a signed bridleway, enjoying superb views to the right as you begin, and now proceed along an excellent track, descending all the while in a south-easterly direction and veering right to reach Old Mill Farm. You veer left through lovely woodland and across a stream with the sound of a waterfall nearby, then veer right; gaining height gradually, you emerge from the woods and veer left, climbing to Home Farm. Veering right again here, you now follow a metalled lane to enter the outskirts of Crowborough.

Cross over Fielden Road and shortly reach another road junction, here turning right into Melfort Road, arriving at the A26. Here you could detour to the Blue Anchor pub just up the A26 to the left, but the continuous route turns right at the end of Melfort Road to follow the A26 briefly. Shortly beyond the house Timbers on the right, look out for a sign for a left turn 150yds ahead and a signed footpath hereabouts to the left. Cross over to follow this footpath soon reaching South View Road and detouring right to enjoy, in 200 yards or so, superb views across

Crowborough Beacon golf course. Then backtrack along South View Road but continue along it this time, noting the impressive Harecombe Manor and more tremendous views between the houses. At the crossroads go straight over into Myrtle Road, turning right into Church Street and following it downhill, with All Saints Church to the left; I suggest you walk along the opposite side, along the left edge of the picturesque Chapel Green, then passing the White Hart pub and reaching a T-junction. Turn right onto a road which soon passes a useful couple of shops and proceeds downhill for about a mile to reach more shops, pub and café at Jarvis Brook. Just before the railway bridge turn right up the station approach road to reach Crowborough station.

Chichester *(Line A, 2.5 miles, circular walk: easy)*

Turn left out of the station approach and pass the Globe pub, crossing over the Avenue de Chartres and continuing on up South Street which boasts a number of eye catching buildings; on your right as you go up, just past Theatre Lane, is No 43, a splendid redbrick building dating from 1792 and formerly a theatre. Next door, no 44, is a fine flint building from around 1820, and just beyond that is the Wren-style Regnum Club that has 18th century features. On the left is the fine Canon Gate, a gatehouse in late Perpendicular style that was largely reconstructed in 1894. Further up, on the same side, is the brick and flint-built Vicar's Hall, given to Chichester Cathedral for the use of the Vicars in 1394; it stands immediately above the Crypt, a late 12th century vaulted undercroft.

Continue on to the Cross, built in 1501 by Bishop Edward Story to enable market traders in the city to sell their goods under cover, and since then it's been used not only for trading but the making of public proclamations.Turn right here into East Street then take the first turning on the left into St Martin's Street, passing the splendid redbrick St Martin's Tea Rooms (one of a huge number of excellent cafes in the city) which are on your left. Soon bear left into Lion Street but you should detour to inspect the pretty St Martin's Square immediately beyond, containing the entrance to St Mary's Hospital and almshouses. Now follow Lion Street westwards to its junction with North Street onto which you turn left. Immediately on the left stands the redbrick and pillared Council House, built in 1731. Continue past the flint-fronted St Olave's Church, now a Christian bookshop, with 13th and 14th century features, and further down on the left is Market House also known as the Buttermarket. Built by Nash in 1807, it's been beautifully restored in recent years with several upmarket shops. Proceed on down to the Cross and this time turn right into West Street.

The cathedral with its magnificent spire now comes into full view on your left. Meanwhile on your right as you follow West Street is a row of shops which occupy the site of the former Dolphin & Anchor Hotel, the buildings of which date back to the 18th and early 19th century. A little further down, past the post office, you reach House of Fraser store, once a school – you can see the motto VIS ET SAPENTIA inscribed towards the top of the building – and opposite you'll observe the Cathedral bell-tower, thought to date from around 1428. Cross to the south side of West Street and pass the bell-tower, then turn left, descend some steps and walk across a wide paved area past the west door of the 11th century cathedral. The cathedral has many treasures: Norman sculptures, magnificent 14th century choirstalls, the imposing 15th century Arundel screen, the shrine of St Richard of Chichester, John Piper's altar tapestry and Marc Chagall's stained glass window depicting Psalm 150.

Continue round from the west door into the cloister, bearing right, then just before the cathedral shop/restaurant, turn right down St Richard's Walk. No 1, immediately on the left, disguises a medieval structure and is probably 14th century. Follow St Richard's Walk to its junction with Canon Lane, the 18th century Deanery facing you as you reach the junction. Your route is to the right but you may wish to detour left to inspect the 13th century Chantry and another alleyway, the Vicars Close, consisting of 15th century houses. Having turned right into Canon Lane from St Richard's Walk, continue to its end, go under the archway and veer left as signed to enter Bishops Palace Gardens. Before doing so you should pause to admire the 13th century flint and brick palace itself, situated on your right. Now keeping to the signed path, you pass under an archway to enter

Chichester old & new; 11th century Cathedral and 21st century Novium

the gardens, following a metalled path through a lovely flower garden; at the far end bear left and then right under the archway to enter a larger area of garden. Go along the obvious path up to the water feature, veering right here to reach a T-junction of paths, turning left here; bear left at the next T-junction and follow it to exit the garden, arriving at the busy Avenue de Chartres. Turn right and almost immediately arrive at a roundabout at which you turn right into West Street, passing the splendid 17th century Edes House that's on your left. A little further up on the left is the former church of St Peter the Great, built in the mid-19th century and now a pub.

Turn left into Tower Street, passing the brand new Novium building housing the city museum and information centre, and opposite the library turn right into the Woolstaplers, bearing left at the T-junction to follow Chapel Street past Providence Chapel, built in 1809, to the left. You shortly arrive at a T-junction with North Walls. Cross over and climb the steps leading onto the walls, parts dating back to 100 AD. Follow them eastwards enjoying good views down to the backs of the neat terraced cottages of Orchard Street, with houses painted green, white and red. You soon arrive at the junction of North Walls with North Street. Cross straight over North Street and proceed along Priory Road; as it bends sharp right, take a path left to return onto the walls, and continue along the walls with Priory Park immediately to your right. In the middle of the park is the former chapel to the 13th century Greyfriars monastery, to your left are the colourful painted stonework of the houses of Franklin Place, and there's a good view of the cathedral spire. At the end drop down to Priory Road; turn right and then left into Little London with its delightful assembly of predominantly redbrick 18th century houses.

Continue down Little London to its junction with East Street, noting immediately opposite the six-column Greek Doric portico of the former Corn Exchange, built in 1832. Turn right into East Street then shortly turn right up a signed alleyway leading to the former (13th century) church of St Andrew Oxmarket. From here you can detour further across the car park in front of you round to the right of the wall and to obtain an excellent view northwards to St Mary's Hospital and chapel. The building has served as a hospital since it was vacated by the Franciscans in 1269. Return to East Street, follow it westwards towards the Cross, and turn left into North Pallant. This contains many fine town houses, with arguably the grandest being the 18th century Pallant House on the left. Its modern neighbour, actually joined to the original Pallant House, is a gallery containing a splendid collection of 20th century British art. Now turn left along East Pallant, noting especially the yellow-painted East Pallant Cottage, then go straight on along New

Town, up to the T-junction with St John's Street.

Turn left here, passing St John's Chapel which is to your right. Built in 1812-13, its features include a gallery and three-decker pulpit, and although it's redundant as a place of worship, it's often open to visitors. Follow the street to its end, turning right into East Street and shortly left into East Walls. Follow the wall parallel with this street, from which there's a good view to the attractive houses of East Row to the left. Descend the steps and turn left into Priory Road, passing the turnings into Little London and St Peter's then bear left along Guildhall Street, noting the impressive former Ship Hotel to your right. At the end turn left into North Street, following it down to the Cross. Look out for two gems on the right, the flint-built Jack Wills shop and No 37 which boasts a fine bay window, while to the left is the imposing Old Cross Inn. Having reached the Cross, go straight down South Street, turning left into West Pallant. On the left is another redundant church, the 13th century All Saints In The Pallant, and No 5, built in about 1770; No 12, on the opposite side, dates back to the early 18th century. At the crossroads turn right into South Pallant then swing round to the right along Old Market Avenue, keeping the modern redbrick Christ Church to your left. At the end turn left and follow South Street back to cross the Avenue de Chartres, continuing in the same direction to reach the station.

Christ's Hospital *(Line A, 11 miles, circular walk: moderate)*

Exit the station, walking via the car park on up Station Road, going straight on into King Edward Road. Shortly bear right across the railway into a continuation of Christ's Hospital Road, now on the course of the Downs Link (DL) footpath, then walk to a T-junction, turning right onto Westons Hill and following it past Westons Farm to a left bend. Turn right here to reach Baystones Bridge, an overbridge crossing of the old Horsham-Guildford railway line; cross the bridge and almost immediately bear hard left as DL signed, passing the bridge which is to your left, then veering right.

From here you follow an excellent well-signposted path past Slinfold along the old line's course, observing the DL signposting throughout. The line opened in 1865 but was a victim of the Beeching axe, and closed in 1965; almost all of it has now been converted into a very scenic footpath/cycleway. Initially the surroundings are pleasantly rural, but even when after a mile and a half you pass the housing and industrial development of Slinfold, going under the A29, the walking remains agreeable and very easy. Beyond Slinfold the path is particularly attractive, passing lovely unspoilt woodland, with perhaps the climax coming with the impressive

and very picturesque underbridge crossing of the river Arun. You need to drop down the steps (actually signed "View Point") to see it properly. It's a double bridge, the original brick bridge not acceptable to the Board of Trade because the gradient required for the line to drop down to it

Victorian splendour at Christ's Hospital school

would have been too great. Continuing on the old line beyond the double bridge, you cross the busy A281, and continue to Rudgwick. The large overbridge you reach a few hundred yards beyond the A281 carries the village street.

Continue along the course of the old line beyond Rudgwick until you get within sight of the 381-yard Baynards Tunnel, marking the summit of the old line. Now you're directed away from the old line, veering off to the left up the hillside, a lovely piece of woodland walking. You arrive at a footpath junction at which you turn right to join the Sussex Border Path, following it clearly signed heading out into the field, just north of east. At the next field boundary you veer to the right and follow the right-hand field edge which skirts the edge of some claypit workings, veering first south-east then north-east, reaching the corner of woodland and veering to the right through the top edge of the woods. Ignoring paths going away to the left, you now proceed south-eastwards as signed across a field to reach the main street at Rudgwick. Turn right past (or possibly into) the pub and walk the short distance down to the church of the Holy Trinity, chiefly 14th century albeit with an early 13th century west tower and a 12th century font made of Sussex marble.

Now continue downhill into the very pretty village centre. Just beyond the village store, turn right down Station Road past the Medical Centre; at the bottom of the road bear left to return to the DL, and turn left to retrace your steps, crossing the A281 and passing the link path to the double bridge (with View Point sign). A mile or so beyond this link path you reach a brick overbridge. Turn left immediately beyond it up steps to meet a bridleway and turn right along it through attractive woodland, soon veering right with the bridleway to reach the A29. Cross straight over it into Park Street and follow it, veering left into The Street and passing through the lovely village of Slinfold, dominated by its large Victorian church but with many fine buildings including the popular Red Lyon (sic) pub. At the time of writing there was also a general store. At the church the village street veers right (southwards), reaching a junction with Lyons Road; go straight on down Hayes Lane. Follow the lane then a short way beyond Streetfield Road to the left, bear left beside Six Acres onto the signed West Sussex Literary Trail. Follow the footpath eastwards then veer right with the path, before branching left as signed, still on the Literary Trail, to arrive back at the DL. Turn left to retrace your steps along the course of the old line for roughly a mile and a half, as far as Baystones Bridge.

Now you have a choice. It's possible for you to continue along the course of the old line for just over half a mile. You arrive close to the extant railway line and reach a signboard (1) which states that walkers need to retrace their steps to Baystones Bridge, but it's possible to veer left here on a well-defined path (not a public right of way), steeply downhill through lovely woodland, then steeply uphill and downhill again to reach a T-junction with a public footpath. Turn right here and soon pass under the railway bridge, veering right and walking up to a T-junction with a driveway. Turn left and follow the driveway briefly to a junction (2) with a path going off to the left, offering "Pedestrian access to Christ's Hospital." If you wish to visit Christ's Hospital school, follow the path uphill and go forward along a metalled road to a T-junction with Christ's Hospital Road, getting an excellent view to the school. To get up close, bear left along Christ's Hospital Road as far as the main school entrance, bearing right into the school grounds and following the driveway as signed; it would be prudent to check in with reception and ask permission to have a wander round the exterior of the buildings. The school was founded in London in 1553, moving here in the 19th century, although some ornamental sections were re-used from the original buildings. They're worth seeing more for their scale and size, and their ambience, rather than for their architectural merit. Now retrace your steps to (2) and turn left (if you haven't detoured, simply keep straight on), almost immediately arriving at the entrance to the station car park, and bearing right to return to the station.

However, from the signboard marked (1) above there's no right of way to the next path T-junction (and no "short cut" access to Christ's Hospital station). If you prefer, then from Baystones Bridge you could follow the DL signposting by leaving the old line as signed, turning hard right over Baystones Bridge and retracing your steps back to the start as on the outward journey, remembering to bear left into King Edward Road after crossing the railway. If you wish to detour to the school, follow King Edward Road round to the right (it becomes Christ's Hospital Road) and keep walking as far as the main entrance. To return to the station, retrace your steps to a smaller (locked) gateway on the bend in the road which is to the left; directly opposite, bear right onto a road which becomes a path, going downhill to arrive at a driveway. Turn left then almost immediately right to the station via the car park.

Collington *(Line C, 1.5 miles, linear walk to Bexhill: easy)*

From the south station exit, walk down Richmond Road to West Parade, going straight over to join the Bexhill seafront promenade. Turn left to follow the promenade eastwards, soon reaching a very impressive clocktower in the middle of West Parade. You can detour briefly inland up Park Avenue behind the clocktower to reach the splendid Bexhill Museum which contains excellent displays relating to the motor racing for which the town became well known in the early 20th century. Now continue along the promenade and soon reach the unmissable De La Warr Pavilion, the first public building in the United Kingdom designed in Modernist style. It was commissioned in 1935 by the Earl De La Warr and envisaged as a "palace of culture" featuring white walls, wooden floors and a floating steel staircase, and included a dance floor and restaurant. Today it boasts galleries, restaurants and a roof terrace amongst its many attractions. It's worth detouring across the green to the pavilion and then going back to the promenade via the ornate viewing platform with tremendous views down the coast towards Eastbourne and Beachy Head. Keep along the promenade, passing a row of houses separated from the

Bexhill's crowning glory, the De La Warr Pavilion

promenade by attractive gardens, and arrive at Channel View East where the promenade veers round to the left. Bear left again beside the coast road, known here as Marina, with beautifully kept gardens on the sea side of the road. Cross over to turn right into Devonshire Road, Bexhill's main shopping area with numerous eateries, and bear right into St Leonards Road which has a quite old-fashioned feel with its many independent stores. Turn left at the end into Sea Road, soon arriving at Bexhill station which is to the left. The Bexhill station walk proceeds on up Sea Road.

Cooden Beach
(Line C, 2.5 miles, circular walk: easy)
Turn left out of the main station entrance up the B2182 Cooden Sea Road, passing Cooden Beach Golf Club, one of the south coast's finest links courses, which is to your left. Shortly beyond the course, turn left into Clavering Walk, and

Low tide showing off Cooden Beach at its most extensive

then second right into Maple Walk. Just beyond Midway Cottage turn left along a plinth-signed path; veer right with the path, keeping houses to your right, and shortly enter an area of woodland. You follow the path north-westwards through the attractive woods, passing just to the left of the medieval Cooden Moat which apparently surrounded the now non-existent Cooden Manor. At the end of the woods you cross a footbridge (1) and arrive at a meadow, with Cooden Wood to your half-left. Cross the meadow and bear left to follow the southern edge of the woods, enjoying good views ahead; beyond the woods, continue across a field in the same direction and arrive at a farm track. Turn right to follow the track uphill.

As you reach the top of the rise, another track comes in from your left and you veer right, soon reaching two barns at the entrance to a very fine flint and brick farmhouse. Just by the first barn, turn right along the left-hand edge of an area of grass, with trees to your left. At the corner, you veer left to pass along the bottom edge of a trim area of green from which there are superb views to the Pevensey Levels, Eastbourne and Beachy Head. At the far corner you continue in the same direction, now skirting the top end of Cooden Wood and keep on the path which now heads just east of south along the edge of the wood, with a field used by caravans to your left. You arrive back at the meadow mentioned above and cross it to return to the footbridge at (1) above. Cross it then almost immediately bear left along an unsigned and narrow but clear path through the wood past the top corner of Cooden Moat, emerging at a new housing development. Go forward onto the road through it, which goes uphill to reach a T-junction with Maple Walk. Turn right to follow it back to Clavering Walk, bearing left here and retracing your steps to the station. This time, however, pass under the railway bridge to arrive at Cooden Beach itself. Try to coincide your visit with a low tide so you can see the magnificent expanse of sand below the shingle, as well as enjoy the views back to Eastbourne and the hills behind. Immediately to your right as you approach the beach is the plush Cooden Beach Hotel, which houses the Motoring Heritage Gallery, a photographic exhibition commemorating the ambition of the then Earl de la Warr to turn Bexhill into the motor racing capital of England in the early 20th century. Then walk back to the station.

Cooksbridge *(Line F, 3.5 miles, linear walk to Lewes: easy)*

Follow the A275 from the station very briefly southwards (signposted Lewes), then just beyond the house Ferndale turn left onto a path which you follow eastwards, crossing over a residential road, and arriving at a field, turn half-right across the field to reach a railway crossing. Cross with care, then bear right to walk beside the railway uphill on a right-hand field edge. You climb to reach a field boundary and immediately beyond that boundary bear left, as signed, along a left-hand field edge, enjoying splendid views to Cliffe Hill beyond Lewes, and, to the right, Offham church with the impressive backcloth of Mount Harry behind. You arrive at a field corner, veering very slightly right into the next field, aiming just to the right of the right-hand redbrick gate post of the splendid Hamsey Manor, also of redbrick! You cross the field then as you get close to Hamsey Lane you join a clearer path on a right-hand field edge that takes you to the road. Turn right then almost immediately left into Whitfeld Lane through the village of Hamsey, past several beautiful houses and barns. The road reaches the bank of the Ouse and bends sharp right, reaching a T-junction (1) with Ivors Lane to the right and the buildings of Hamsey Place to the left. Your way is straight on, along the right bank of the river, but it's worth detouring to the left and following the lane uphill over the long-defunct Lewes-Uckfield line and reaching the Norman church of St Peter. Even if it isn't open you can enjoy the exterior and exquisite setting.

Return to the junction at (1) and now go forward along the bank of the Ouse all the way to Lewes. It's very straightforward, if muddy in places, usually with a choice of an embankment path or the bank itself. The views to Offham church and Mount Harry to the right, and Hamsey church to the left, remain excellent.

Just over a mile from (1) above you reach a bridge, the first bridge over the river you'll have seen since Hamsey. Turn left to cross the bridge and shortly bear right onto a path which proceeds close to the left bank, then, beyond Tesco store, goes down to the water's edge and passes under a road bridge. Beyond the bridge, you're directed left then shortly right, past a car park along a narrow alley to the pretty High Street of the district of Cliffe. Turn right to follow the street past Harveys Brewery, established in 1790; go back over the Ouse and forward to cross Eastgate Street. Go straight up the hill, now back on Lewes High Street, arriving at the very impressive war memorial, then, keeping to the left pavement, continue briefly to a crossroads junction with Station Street and Fisher Street. Turn left down Station Street and shortly arrive back at the station which is on the left.

Crawley *(Line A, 2 miles, circular walk: easy)*

Turn left out of the main station entrance and follow Station Way westwards, soon reaching the A2219 Brighton Road. Bear left and go across the level crossing, turning immediately right into Springfield Road, following it to a T-junction with the A2220 Horsham Road. Cross and turn left to follow it very briefly, then turn right through the main entrance of Goffs Park. You pass a useful information board, then shortly turn left along a path (signed "toilets") uphill, keeping the park's eastern boundary immediately to the left. You're now on the park's "red route" which you'll follow throughout your time in the park; simply follow the red arrows! Climb up, keeping to your right the impressive Goffspark House which now houses Crawley Museum. Go round the left side of the mansion into its car park and follow the approach road to view the fine old Goffs Manor, now a popular pub but once the home of actor Peter Vaughan (who played "Genial" Harry Grout in *Porridge*!). Retrace your steps back towards Goffspark House but now bear left on a path which aims for and passes another useful information board. Red route signposting is excellent as you describe a semi-circle round the park's lovely lake in the shade of woodland, looking out for grey squirrels, willow warblers and great spotted woodpeckers.

  Having completed the semi-circle, bear left as (red) signed and walk downhill past a children's play area to a T-junction with the wide tarmac track through the centre of the park. Turn left to follow it, until you reach a pitch-and-putt golf course, turning right along a path which follows a line of thin trees, heading for the railway beyond the park. Turn right at the bottom to follow the path along the (northern) end of the park, passing a dinky miniature railway and exiting the park. Now bear left to follow Horsham Road over the level crossing, bearing right almost immediately beyond the crossing into Spencers Road which takes you to the Asda car park, and

The Old Punch Bowl; an old pub in a New Town

walk towards the store entrance. However before reaching it, veer left, following the Asda exit road which arrives just south-east of the Grand Parade roundabout. Cross over the road using the crossing, and go forward along a road to a T-junction with the attractive and historic High Street now dominated by pubs and restaurants rather than shops. Turn left to pass the 15th century George and go down to the end of the street, crossing over and bearing left to inspect the splendid timber-framed Old Punch Bowl, a 15th century building, where a farm once stood. Now head back up the High Street passing the 14th century Brewery, the mainly 18th century White Hart, Crawley's first post office, and No 49-51, which with its fine timberframing dates back to 1440. Continue to Church Walk and turn left to follow this attractive narrow alley to arrive at St John's church. Founded in 1250, its tower was mostly built in the 15th century, and the pulpit dates from 1627. One of the windows in the northern aisle celebrates Mark Lemon, the first editor of Punch magazine, who lived in the High Street. Whether you've visited the church, pass to the left (north) side of it, going forward into Haslett Avenue West and following it to just short of the County Mall. To return to the station, simply turn right by McDonald's and follow Friary Way back to the station, but for the town centre go straight on, keeping the County Mall indoor shopping area to the right, turning left and walking down to Queens Square. Here you'll find the town bandstand, originally erected at Gatwick and moved to its present site in 1958 when the airport opened. From here, retrace your steps to just past County Mall and then turn left to follow Friary Way to the station.

Crowborough *(Line G, 8 miles, circular walk: moderate)*

Turn right out of the station exit and right again onto the B2100 Rotherfield Road, passing under the bridge then following the B2100 all the way to Rotherfield. There's pavement initially but then that peters out, and after a roadside walk – take care of passing traffic – you then have a stiff climb up the hill on which Rotherfield is built, albeit with attractive houses lining the road as you ascend. As you get level with the parish church of St Denys which is to the right, turn right to visit this superb building, which boasts box pews, Jacobean pulpit and fine carved screen between side chapel and chancel. Return to the B2100 and follow it to the village centre, passing (and perhaps visiting) the Catt Inn on the other side. Cross the road and turn right along the High Street, crossing Station Road and passing the adjacent pub, then turning left onto a path hard to the right of the pub. Follow the path which soon crosses New Road and goes straight over along Horsegrove Road; at its end you reach a path fork, bearing right downhill along a right-hand field edge to reach a path junction. Here you bear left, south-eastwards, walking down the hillside, entering an area of woodland and following it in the same direction. Observing the signposts, you emerge from the wood and climb, veering left as signed to reach a farm lane, turning right to shortly arrive at Sheriff's Lane.

Turn right to follow it to a T-junction with the B2101, turning left and following it for just over a quarter of a mile, then as the road bends gently left, bear right along a narrow road which climbs steeply to Argos Hill. You reach a crossroads of lanes at the top, detouring hard left here to shortly enjoy a fantastic view to the north. Return to the crossroads and turn left, passing Argos Hill windmill, a post mill dating back to about 1835, while from the other side of the road there's an excellent view to the buildings of Mayfield. Continue on along the road which begins to drop steeply, but shortly before reaching the A267 turn right onto a signed bridleway; follow it to Pages Farm, then continue along it, veering sharp right and then left to reach Fir Toll Road (1). Turn left to follow it to the A267, crossing straight over and climbing to arrive at a crossroads junction with Love Lane and Stone Cross. Go straight over onto Station Road and then High Street to reach the centre of Mayfield with its many refreshment opportunities. Mayfield

Black and white beauty; Mayfield's splendid Middle House

is a lovely village with many beautiful buildings on its main street, arguably none more so than the timber-framed Middle House Hotel which dates back to 1576. By continuing to the top end of the High Street and veering left, you immediately reach the entrance to St Leonards RC convent which incorporates the remains of the medieval Archbishops Palace, the 14th century great hall of which survives and is now used as a chapel. There's apparently nothing to stop you going into the grounds, but you should go to the well-signed reception area and ask for permission to explore. The first of a number of Archbishops of Canterbury to live here was St Dunstan to whom the parish church, with its Jacobean pulpit and 17th century octagonal font, is dedicated. If you've time, the car park off the south side of the main street offers a fantastic view to the countryside south of the village.

Retrace your steps to (1) and continue along Fir Toll Road for a couple of hundred yards, turning right as signed along a footpath going parallel with the road and arriving at a lane; turn right to follow the lane just west of north, veering north-westwards as signed along an overgrown path, downhill. You then emerge to ascend in the same direction along a right-hand field edge, passing the edge of a wood and then contouring the hillside in the next field, a little way up from the left-hand edge, to enter an area of woodland. Follow through this to reach Argos Hill Road, turning left to follow it briefly then shortly bear right as signed along a path through more trees, just west of north. At the far end, go through a gate and turn left to follow a left-hand field edge, rising to a field boundary and here veering right across the field, turning right to follow Five Ashes Road uphill to a T-junction with Mayfield Road, turning right along it briefly. Soon turn left to follow Peeps Lane past houses, going forward in the same direction along a clearly signed bridleway which arrives at Dewlands Manor Golf Club. The bridleway peters out as you continue across the course; you pass (but don't take) a signed path going off to the right but very shortly beyond that you turn sharp left as signed across a fairway. Beyond the fairway crossing turn right along what is now a very clear path, initially beside the golf course and uphill, north-westwards; you then begin to descend, following the obvious path all the way down to the B2100 Rotherfield Road. Turn left to follow it, soon veering right to pass under the railway bridge, shortly then turning left to reach Crowborough station.

Crowhurst *(Line H, 4 miles, linear walk to Battle: moderate)*

Exit the station on the south side and follow Station Road to its end; go more or less straight over into the churchyard and walk up the main church path. To your left is a huge and ancient yew tree, and views through the trees to the remains of the late 13th century Manor House. Continue past the door of the church, which contains some 13th century work, and follow the path round to the right, up through the churchyard to a gate. Beyond the gate, turn left to follow the road briefly, then as the road veers right, go straight on along the signed 1066 Country Walk (Bexhill Link). Initially you follow a right-hand field edge with houses to the right, then continue in a straight line along a clear field path and straight on down through the trees to another field. Veer gently right here as signed, gently rising through the field to the entrance to the Fore Wood RSPB Nature Reserve which enjoys a huge variety of birds. Continue along an obvious path through the wood, going to the left of the pond and descending to a signed path junction where you need to fork right along the 1066 route, then

Part of Crowhurst's ruined Manor House

ascend before dropping down again. The path veers sharply left and exits the wood, crossing a field; bear right at a path junction at the edge of another area of woodland and walk through the woods to reach a path crossroads beside a delightful cottage.

Turn right at this crossroads along a lane, descending past houses to reach the picturesquely named Peppering Eye Farm complex, with its very striking tile-hung buildings including a tastefully converted oast house. Bear left at its end into Telham Lane, almost immediately reaching a junction with Powdermill Lane, B2095. Carefully cross straight over onto a path which runs parallel with the road, northwards. As the road veers sharply right you continue straight on with the 1066 route, crossing a lane and joining a good wide track heading downhill. Within the parkland to your right is the site of the Battle of Hastings, and the ruins of Battle Abbey and its surrounding buildings are clearly visible behind. Having reached the hill bottom, go straight on along a fairly clear path uphill on a right-hand field edge. At length you reach a junction with the "main" 1066 Country Walk route. Turn right along what is a really excellent path, with woodland to your right, and having passed the abbey car park, continue to arrive in the very centre of Battle, by the entrance to the gatehouse and the abbey. To pick up and continue with the described Battle station walk from here (you won't miss anything you would otherwise have seen!), proceed north-westwards up the High Street past the Pilgrims Rest. Otherwise, turn right onto the main street beyond the gatehouse, passing St Mary's church which is to the left; shortly then turn right into Lower Lake and descend, then just beyond the B2095 junction, bear left into Station Approach and follow it to Battle station.

Doleham - *see Three Oaks (page 152)*

Durrington-on-Sea *(Line B, 4 miles, linear walk to Goring-by-Sea: easy)*

Leave the station by the main exit, turning immediately right and walking beside the railway to a flight of steps taking you up to Shaftesbury Avenue. Turn right and follow it to a T-junction with the A259 which you cross, turning left and bearing almost immediately right into Sea Place which you follow all the way to the beach and the concrete coast path. I recommend that you go across the coast path and round the far side of the beach huts onto the shingle, turning right and following the shingle westwards. Looking back there are excellent views to Worthing pier and well beyond to the cliffs east of Brighton and towards the Seven Sisters. When the huts relent, cut across the shingle to pick up the coast path (maybe detouring to a tempting café to the right), joining the coast path just before it veers right through trees. Now a stony track, it emerges from the trees and follows a charming course with a greensward to your right and the sea to your left. Beyond a toilet

Part of the attractive Ilex Way en route for Goring Hall

block, continue along the path at the back of the beach, with the lovely open space of Goring Gap to the right and splendid views to Highdown Hill beyond. At the west end of the green, bear right to head north along the concrete path parallel with Sea Lane. As you approach the end of the open area on the right, turn right along a signed bridleway, Ilex Way, an avenue created in the 1840s by the Lyon family to provide carriage access to their home at Goring Hall. It's now a haven of wildlife including bats, beetles, shrews, foxes, squirrels and hedgehogs, a wide variety of birds and butterflies, and plants including the red campion and hairy violet. Opposite house number 49, you could detour through a gate across Fernhurst Recreation Ground to its far corner, going straight over into an adjacent field; by turning hard left into this second field beside the flint wall, you will at the far end get a superb view to the red-brick Goring Hall, now part of a hospital. You could then return to Ilex Way via the right-hand (eastern) edge of the recreation ground.

Whether you've detoured or not, follow Ilex Way parallel with Fernhurst Drive, but very shortly beyond the recreation ground leave the avenue to veer left with the road and then right at the T-junction which very shortly follows. You then turn almost immediately left into Goring Street, by the lovely flint and brick Bulls Head pub which is on the corner. Follow Goring Street to a T-junction with Goring Way, turning right onto it then immediately left to continue along Goring Street to the level crossing. Goring-by-Sea station is immediately to the right here.

Eastbourne *(Line C, 3.5 miles, circular walk: easy)*

From the front of the station bear left to make your way along Terminus Road into the main shopping area, passing the Arndale Centre, then at Marks & Spencer turn right to continue along Terminus Road and this brings you to the seafront. Cross over and turn left to follow the upper promenade beside Grand Parade, enjoying the magnificent Carpet Gardens, established in the town for over a century, and the very impressive architecture. You pass, or perhaps detour to wander along, the pier, built in 1872, then continue along the promenade, reaching the Redoubt, part of Eastbourne's coastal defence against the threat of Napoleonic invasion, completed in 1803. It is now the Sussex Combined Services Museum, featuring a history of the Royal Sussex Regiment which was founded in 1701. Retrace your steps to the pier and now follow Grand Parade as far as Devonshire Place, turning right to follow it to a roundabout junction with South Street. Bear immediately left into Cornfield Terrace to visit the How We Lived Then Museum Of Shops giving a glimpse of what shopping was like in days gone by, containing around 75,000 exhibits.

Continue beyond the museum along Cornfield Terrace, turning shortly left into Burlington Place, then at the next crossroads turn right into Compton Street. Follow it to its junction with Carlisle Place to the left, noting to your right the Devonshire Park Theatre and Winter Gardens, then turn hard left into Carlisle Place which has a distinctly Italian feel. You reach the coast road here, crossing over and walking down to the popular RNLI Lifeboat Museum, going on to the conspicuous Wish Tower – one of the Martello towers erected in the Napoleonic Wars – then make your way to the upper seafront promenade, turning right to follow it briefly. Enjoying lovely views to Beachy Head you now follow beside Western Lawns which are to the right and as you get level with the Duke of Devonshire statue turn right to pass it and return to the coast road. Cross over within sight of the magnificent white-fronted Grand Hotel which dates back to 1875 and whose guests have included Winston Churchill and Charlie Chaplin. Walk briefly back towards the Lifeboat Museum but on the inland side of the coast road, soon turning left into Wilmington Square. At its far end is the unmissable Congress Theatre and immediately to its left is the Towner, a very impressive art gallery with a spectacular interior. Make your way to the gallery then bear round to the left of it to enter College Road northwards; to your right is the Devonshire Park tennis centre, which attracts some of the world's finest lady players to a pre-Wimbledon tournament. At the top end of College Road kink briefly right into Furness Road and almost immediately reach South Street. To your right is the massive red brick church of St Saviour, dating back to 1867, but you turn left into South Street through an area known as Little Chelsea with an interesting individual mix of shops and eateries. At the far end you reach Grove Road, crossing over to reach the huge Town Hall, built of brick and Portland stone in the mid-1880s.

Bear left onto Grove Road then immediately right up Saffrons Road, then at its end, cross over Dittons Road and go straight on into Gildredge Park. Follow the path in the same direction, then just beyond a line of trees to the left, strike out across the green to the left hand corner of the enclosed park ahead (you may of course be tempted by the café to the right of the park!). Walk beside the park railings in the same direction, pass through the gate and walk a few steps, then turn left onto a metalled path. Shortly fork right onto a path that goes parallel with a tennis court and veers a little left, keeping a charming flower garden to your right, rising to reach a yellow-painted thatched house known as the Hermitage. Turn right here onto a path that leads to a T-junction with another path, going straight over and crossing the green, keeping the redbrick 18th century Manor House just to your left. At the end of the green descend the steps to arrive at the A259 and the heart of the Old Town. Cross over and bear left, passing the sensational timber-framed Lamb Inn, parts of which date back to the 12th century, crossing Ocklynge Road and entering the churchyard of St Mary's. Follow the path aiming for and skirting the north side of the church, to pass the superb 16th century flint Old Parsonage, then carry on along the path reach to Church Lane. Turn left at the end to follow it back to the A259 and left again to the main entrance to the church of St Mary the Virgin.

Having visited the church, cross over the road and continue on along the right side of the A259 to the end of Borough Lane. It's worth detouring very briefly up the lane to view, on the right,

The fine flint-built Parsonage in the heart of Eastbourne's old town

the lovely timber-framed 16th century Pilgrim House where Charles Dickens occasionally stayed, and a fine brick 18th century house immediately adjacent. Now return to the A259 and this time carry on down the A259 (The Goffs) then within sight of the T-junction at the end, bear right onto Southfields Road, following it to its end at a roundabout. Follow the roundabout round, crossing Old Orchard Road and Grove Road, then cross the A259 to arrive back at the station.

East Grinstead *(Line J, 6 miles, circular walk: moderate)*

Walk from the station down the Sainsbury's approach road and go straight over the roundabout along Railway Approach, following it to its end and turning right onto London Road. Very shortly turn left onto King Street and immediately right up Institute Walk; follow this in a straight line, turning right into Cantelupe Road, and following it to the High Street, passing or visiting the town's smart museum. Turn left into the High Street then soon left through the churchyard; the sandstone church of St Swithun was built just a couple of centuries ago and has eight bells, the largest peal in Sussex. Exit the churchyard through the lychgate and turn right down Church Lane to return to the High Street. To make progress you cross and turn right towards the Dorset Arms, but you should look half-left to the superb half-timbered Cromwell House, dating from the 12th century, and turn hard left for the entrance to Sackville College; founded by the Earl of Dorset in the early 17th century, it's a set of almshouses built round a graceful quadrangle. Now walk along the High Street past the eight-bayed 18th century Dorset Arms, then follow the narrow street parallel with the High Street, continuing along the south side of the High Street. There are numerous very fine timber-framed houses, with a number of excellent shops including a particularly good bookshop. Go forward past the splendid timber-framed Clarendon House which is to the left, to the mini-roundabout junction with Ship Street.

Turn left into Ship Street and follow it southwards, veering right at a mini-roundabout and going forward along Dunning's Road downhill out of the town. Pass the attractive Old Mill pub, then begin to rise, going past an arts centre and continuing south-westwards uphill until, just over half a mile from the Old Mill pub, you reach a left turn signposted Public Footpath and Standen. Turn left along what is the approach road to Standen, then shortly before cottages on the right, bear right onto the path signed High Weald Landscape Trail (HWLT) to the right, south-westwards – don't take the path going hard right here. You may of course wish to detour to visit Standen: to do this, simply continue downhill past the cottages to arrive at this 19th century National Trust-owned property. It's a remarkable mix of architectural styles, and is regarded as one of the finest houses of Philip Webb, a close associate of William Morris whose designs decorate the house. You then need to backtrack and turn left to join the HWLT.

Having joined the HWLT, follow a clear path alongside the field, with trees to the left, reaching a metalled kissing gate. Go through it and follow the obvious path downhill, veering just east of south, along a left-hand field edge, arriving at a path junction, from which there's a good view to Standen to your left. Take the path signed straight on; don't be lured into the field to the half-left, but rather follow a narrow dirt track on the right side of that field, again in obedience to the HWLT signs. You enter a wood and begin to descend, passing a junction with a path going away to your right (2) by a rather redundant stile. Ignore the next left turn but then shortly beyond that, you reach another path junction (3), a signed path this time going off to your left. Turn left to follow this path, soon emerging from the woods to get a lovely view to the Weir Wood Reservoir, and walk downhill past but not through a gate, along a left-hand field edge, arriving at a stile just beneath pylons. Cross the stile and turn right to follow the Sussex Border Path (SBP) which follows close to the Weir Wood Reservoir, keeping it to the left albeit separated by vegetation. The reservoir is a delightful haven for wildlife, with flocks of mallard and moorhen, and you may be lucky enough to see a curlew.

Shortly the path veers sharp right and goes under pylons again. Leave the SBP here, turning right onto a signed path across a field, getting an excellent view to Standen Rock, one of a number of sandstone outcrops in the Tunbridge Wells/East Grinstead area. You enter the trees and find yourself back at the path junction (3) above. Walk briskly uphill then turn left at (2) along a lovely path through woods, with good views through the trees to the reservoir and the top of Standen Rock. At the end your path swings right to reach a road. Follow it past the Deer Leap cycle complex, then at the fork road junction bear left and follow it for a little over quarter of a mile as far as the entrance to the 18th century stone Saint Hill Manor, home of the Church of Scientology, and open to the public at various times. Retrace your steps briefly then turn left onto a signed bridleway, soon passing a tastefully converted chapel and a lovely brick cottage, Milton Mount. Shortly beyond here you reach a path junction. Turn left, now back on the HWLT, and follow it north-eastwards through a succession of fields, keeping Dunning's Wood to the left. You arrive at an area of buildings, going forward to a T-junction with a drive, turning right as signed to return to Dunning's Road. Turn left onto it briefly, but soon turn left along a signed path, passing the left side of the snooker hall, and then as HWLT-signed through quite thick vegetation. A further signpost reassures you, taking you past the left side of another large building and it's now straightforward going along a narrow but clear path mainly along right-hand field edges, with a stream to your right. You pass a delightful duckpond then kink slightly right to join a narrow path continuing in the same direction that brings you to Turners Hill Road. Cross and turn right to immediately reach a roundabout, turning hard left onto Gardenwood Road and following it under the magnificent ten-arch redbrick Imberhorne Viaduct, carrying the Lewes-East Grinstead railway which opened in 1882.

Ivy-clad Saint Hill Manor

Immediately beyond the viaduct (4) turn right up a metalled path which continues along the right edge of a large housing estate, with the proposed East Grinstead extension of the Bluebell Railway to the right. As the path arrives at the station car park it turns sharp right then left to pass above East Grinstead station and reaches a footbridge. (As a more scenic but lengthier alternative, at (4)

continue along the road uphill, turning right into Dickens Close then left at the end to reach the Worth Way, course of the old Three Bridges-Groombridge line; turn hard right to follow it, getting great views to the viaduct, as far as the station car park, then walk round the far top end of the car park to reach the footbridge.) Cross the bridge then turn right at the bottom to return to the station.

East Worthing *(Line B, 6.5 miles, linear walk to Lancing: moderate)*

Exit the station onto the immediately adjacent B2223 Dominion Road and follow it north-westwards. In just over a quarter of a mile bear right into Southdown View Road, crossing over Harrison Road and going forward, veering sharp left, to arrive at a T-junction with Penfold Road. Bear right here and stay on this road which becomes Northbrook Road, then bear right shortly into Clarendon Road and second left off Clarendon Road into Southways Avenue. At the end, turn right into Bramber Road which soon peters out; at its far left-hand end join a signed footpath which heads half-left, north-eastwards, across a field. You arrive at Upper Brighton Road (B2222) crossing more or less straight over to follow Lambleys Lane northwards, crossing the A27 and then gently gaining height. As the road bends a little to the left after 300 yards or so, take a signed path heading right (eastwards). At its far end turn left up Church Lane, soon reaching Sompting church which is to your left. It boasts England's finest Saxon steeple, built early in the 11th century, although the foundations can be traced back to 960. The Saxon carvings on the arches of the tower interior are among the earliest examples of English architectural carving. The roof is made up of four diamond shaped surfaces meeting in a point; it is known as Rhenish helm, and is unique in England.

Beyond the church, continue along the road past the impressive Sompting Abbotts; the road, now Titch Hill, soon bends sharply right and then shortly left and there's no pavement, so take care. The road rises then drops to the pretty Steepdown Cottage and Titch Hill Farm, and opposite Steepdown Cottage, you turn hard right onto a path which heads south-eastwards to arrive at a T-junction with another path. Turn left here and now head uphill for about a mile. Eventually you reach a T-junction of paths, turning right and very shortly reaching a crossroads of paths, turning right; turn almost immediately right again to join a path which climbs steeply to the summit of Steep Down, marked by a trig point. This is a really superb viewpoint, with views which include the Weald, the South Downs to Truleigh Hill, the Adur valley, Lancing College Chapel, and a vast coastal strip from the cliffs east of Brighton to Butlins at Bognor and even beyond. Beyond the trig point continue along the path south-eastwards, dropping down to a T-junction of paths. Turn left here and almost immediately turning right at the next T-junction to follow a clear path south-eastwards uphill, still enjoying magnificent views to the Adur valley.

Rise to an area of woodland, part of the Lancing Ring Nature Reserve, notable for its chalk grassland, then keep along the path through the trees and start to descend. On your descent, fork right onto an (easily missed) path with a car park just to the right of this path going off to the right here; it becomes a metalled road, descending steeply to a crossroads junction with roads. Go straight across, following Mill Road downhill to a T-junction with Manor Road (there's a welcome pub/restaurant on the corner here) onto which you turn right. This is the centre of North Lancing, which has some delightful buildings of flint, timber and thatch, and on your left along Manor Road you'll see a pretty Saxon/Norman church, St James The Less, containing fine windows. Almost immediately beyond the church turn left down the tranquil Upper West Lane to cross the A27, again with enormous care; using the gap in the fence immediately to the left of the crossing ramp on the far side, go straight on into West Lane and follow it just west of south. At the end cross straight over Crabtree Lane onto a footpath which passes a recreation ground and goes forward to cross Penstone Park, then shortly beyond the crossing the path bends right and arrives at Sompting Road, the B2222. Turn left to follow this road, veering left to arrive at Lancing station which is to the right.

Eridge *(Line G, 11.5 miles, circular walk: strenuous)*

Turn right out of the station and almost immediately turn right onto Forge Road which initially proceeds roughly parallel with the railway but then bends sharp left and then sharp right. Shortly beyond the sharp right turn, bear left onto a metalled lane signed for various properties but also a footpath. Follow the lane through the woods then out into the fields, veering south-westwards. The metalled lane bends sharp right but you carry on along a rough track, very soon reaching a path crossroads by a footbridge. Turn right to follow the path uphill, now on the Sussex Border Path (SBP). The path continues clearly north-westwards past the buildings of Bullfinches, then still heading north-west, begins to descend, passing along the left fringe of an area of woodland. You plunge down to the bottom of the hill then start to ascend, reaching a path fork in the shade of trees. Take the left fork here, leaving the SBP and following the left-hand edge of the field ahead, going steeply uphill to reach a road. Turn left to follow the road westwards, soon veering left to reach the B2188, turning left to follow this road for a little over a quarter of a mile, climbing to reach a fork road junction in woodland, where a road goes off to Crowborough. Immediately opposite this junction turn right onto a signed path which proceeds delightfully through woodland, emerging at the edge of pasture and meeting the High Weald Landscape Trail (HWLT). The right of way turns right here and skirts the woodland to the right, veering left (north-westwards) aiming for a stile in the trees. However by walking to the highest point of the pasture straight ahead you get an excellent view to the early 19th century Buckhurst Park mansion, part of the Buckhurst estate, owned by the Sackvilles since around 1200.

Following the HWLT, enter the trees by the stile as signed, bearing left to follow the path north-westwards along the edge of the woods, turning right at a T-junction with a driveway and following it downhill; veer left and carry on along the drive through Buckhurst Park to reach the B2110 by the weatherboarded Dorset Arms at Withyham. Turn left to follow the road briefly to pass below Withyham church. To visit the church, either turn left onto a signed permissive path which heads steeply up the hill to enter the churchyard (a sign advises the gate into the churchyard is locked on Lady Day and Michelmas Day!) or follow the road a little further then fork left with the HWLT onto a track, then left again onto a metalled lane and left again to the church. The church was rebuilt in the 17th century having been struck by lightning, its undoubted highlight being the chapel with memorial effigies to the Sackville family.

However you've reached the church, descend to the T-junction with the metalled lane referred to above and turn left to follow the HWLT along it; turn right as signed with the HWLT after a couple of hundred yards, going south-westwards across a field to enter a wood. Proceed through the wood, avoiding a left fork at one point, and on emerging from the wood turn right as HWLT-signed to follow the right-hand edge of a field, keeping the buildings of Forstal Farm to your right. Beyond the farm buildings you veer left, just north of west, skirting trees that are to the left and climbing onto a hillside through the middle of a field. HWLT signage reassures you as you continue to a field boundary, crossing a stile to find yourself at the eastern corner of another field, and a path junction.

At this point (1) you have the option of a lengthy detour to Poohsticks Bridge which will add 3 miles to your walk (see footnote below). The main route however sticks to the HWLT and follows the right-hand (bottom) field edge, crosses a stile beside a gate and continues along the right-hand edge of the next field, soon proceeding as signed to cross over into Church Lane. Turn left to pass the church and enter the very attractive village of Hartfield. The church of St Mary boasts a superb lychgate effectively incorporating the upper floor of an adjacent timber-framed cottage dating back to 1520; there are two popular pubs and a shop dedicated to selling Winnie the Pooh memorabilia, Pooh's creator A.A. Milne having lived nearby and based the stories on real places in nearby Ashdown Forest including what has come to be known as Poohsticks Bridge (see below).

A summer's evening on the Forest Way

Walk back up Church Lane, turning left beside the lychgate onto a narrow metalled path heading downhill, then pass just to the left of a school and on to reach a green. Walk across the green along the obvious pathway leading to a gate at the far end, turning right to follow the B2110 briefly then left into Castlefield and right into Mottefield. Shortly a road leads off up to a gate providing the best view to the "motte and bailey" but your route turns off Mottefield just beyond this road, along a narrow metalled path. Cross a stile and now bear round to the right as signed through the meadow, crossing into another field as signed and immediately bearing left along a left-hand field edge, heading north-eastwards. Maintaining the same direction, go forward as signed into another field, arriving at a T-junction with a broad track, the Forest Way, the course of the now defunct East Grinstead-Tunbridge Wells railway. Follow the Forest Way for some 2.5 miles, your straight progress only interrupted by the need to cross the B2110 at Ham Bridge, then as the extant railway comes in from the left you veer right to reach a crossing of the B2188. Cross over, staying on the Forest Way but continuing beside the railway, then veer left to pass under the railway and veer right to go forward to a road. Turn left onto the road, soon veering right. The road veers left by a school (2).

The recommended route goes straight on (to the right of the school) along a path, but to break at Groombridge, veer left to follow the road straight down into the centre of the village; the old village with delightful triangular green, and redbrick Groombridge Place wih splendid gardens, are just beyond the modern village centre. If you wished to shorten your walk you could catch a train to Eridge using the preserved Spa Valley Railway (SVR); to do this, having veered left with the road at (2) above, turn right onto a road in a couple of hundred yards, (opposite the Orchard Rise turning to the left) then at the T-junction of roads, go straight on along a footpath, cross over Station Road and go down steps.

At the bottom go straight on past the old station building then right to access the platform. When part of the main network this line linked Tunbridge Wells with the London-Uckfield line at Eridge and was shut as recently as 1985.

To continue along the recommended route from point (2) towards Eridge, follow the path straight on, soon crossing over the SVR and proceeding south-eastwards to reach a lane at Birchden, turning right onto it and following it downhill through the woods, now on the Tunbridge Wells Circular Walk. Follow the footpath signs, leaving the main track as signed, passing to the left of a car park and arriving at the west end of the woods, with the SVR just across the meadow. Now follow a clear path roughly parallel with the railway, but a gate and signboard to the left allows you to join a path immediately below Harrisons Rocks, part of a number of outcrops of rock just south-west of Tunbridge Wells providing a tremendous training ground for climbers whose activities may entertain you as you pass! In due course the paths merge and you continue south-eastwards to the buildings of Forge Farm; turn right at the footpath junction here as signed, crossing the railway and arriving at Forge Road. Turn left to follow the road for roughly a mile, bearing left again at its end to arrive back at Eridge station.

POOHSTICKS BRIDGE DETOUR: At (1), leave the HWLT, going diagonally uphill across the field, then go forward to follow the right-hand edge of the next field to arrive at a road, the B2026 Jacks Hill. Turn right then left across the green to briefly follow the B2110 Newtons Hill. However in a couple of hundred yards turn left along a signed footpath along a right-hand field edge then through trees. Emerging at the end, turn right to walk past the buildings of Gallipot Hill Farm which are to the right, enjoying stunning views southwards to Ashdown Forest. Beyond the farm, turn left as signed to walk downhill through fields to reach a lane; turn left to follow it southwards, ignoring a lane going off to the left, and proceed pleasantly to Poohsticks Bridge – the bridge at the north end of Ashdown Forest said to have been the birthplace of the Poohsticks game, courtesy of the work of A.A. Milne. It was effectively rebuilt as recently as 1999. Retrace your steps all the way to the B2110 Newtons Hill, turning right but now staying on this road as it veers to the left to reach Hartfield. To rejoin the continuous route, head away from the village street up Church Lane.

Etchingham *(Line H, 5.5 miles, linear walk to Stonegate: easy)*

Walk down the station approach road, turning right onto the A265 High Street, soon reaching the church on the right. This massive 14th century church was the baronial church of Sir William de Echyngham; a fine memorial to him in chainmail lies in front of the altar, while other features of interest in the church include choir stalls with misericords and 15th century brasses. Having visited it, follow the footpath along the right (north-east) side of the church, soon arriving at a road, Church Hill. Turn right to follow it to a junction with Fysie Lane going off to the right. Bear left here along Sheepstreet Lane, ignoring the first bridleway turning going off to the right, but taking the next right path, a couple of hundred yards further on. Follow the path, actually a lane, to Kitchingham Farm, forking left at the fork junction as you reach the buildings. Pass through the farm complex, making sure you fork right beyond the buildings then veer gently left, just east of north, on a lovely path heading uphill along the left edge of trees. At the end you turn left onto the B2099, soon reaching Pashley Manor and gardens to the left. The gardens are among the finest in Sussex and well worth a visit with their blend of fine old trees, fountains, springs and large ponds with tremendous views across the surrounding countryside. In spring there's an abundance of tulips while later months bring lavender, sweet peas, lilies and late-flowering herbaceous perennials. The manor house, not open to the public, dates back to the mid-16th century.

   Continue along the B2099 to Ticehurst, turning left in the village centre down Church Street. Ticehurst is a lovely village with many old weatherboarded and tile-hung cottages, a couple of pubs and several traditional shops; look out for the Coopers sign, indicating one past retail business, the site now occupied by a café. The church of St Mary dates back to the 13th and 14th centuries and contains wooden choir stalls carved by Robert Thompson whose trademark was the addition of lifelike church mice to his carvings. Follow Church Street downhill out of the village, past turnings to Sheepwash Farm and Parsonage Farm then just over half a mile from Ticehurst village centre bear right onto a signed path, going downhill through rough grass to cross a stream. You then ascend, taking care not to miss a path sign leading you into the field to the left, following this field diagonally to its bottom (south-west) end,

A lovely preserved shopfront in Ticehurst

here going forward to a lane and heading straight on along it westwards. Shortly beyond a left bend, bear left onto a signed path, soon veering right as signed onto a clear path through Limden Wood. Emerging at its west end, turn left to climb steeply up through the pasture (no path on the ground) and go forward to a road.

Turn right onto the road then shortly right again onto Cottenden Road to within sight of Stonegate village school. Just before the school turn left onto a signed path which goes steeply downhill through pasture, aiming just to the right of the trees ahead then passing to the right of a sewage works. Shortly beyond the works you veer left, over a stream to a path junction on the east edge of the trees. Take the right path fork which follows the left-hand edge of the woodland then enters the wood; watch carefully for a signed exit and continuation of the path along the right-hand field edge. Just beyond the next field boundary fork right onto a path which drops steeply downhill through the woods. Cross over a plank bridge and go steeply up the other side, veering right to emerge from the trees and left (south-westwards) to pass through further trees. Now entering a field, continue south-westwards to the far (south-west) field corner, then walk diagonally across the next field, arriving at a lane just above the buildings of Hammerden. Turn left onto the lane, then just before the pond to the right you turn hard right onto a path which soon veers left and takes you to Stonegate station.

Falmer *(Line C, 4.5 miles, circular walk: moderate)*

Take the Lewes bound (ticket office) station exit and go down to the subway under the A27, shortly turning hard left onto a concrete cycle path parallel with the A27. Shortly bear right along a metalled road which proceeds very pleasantly beside the Stanmer Park Nature Reserve to reach the green, with Stanmer House on one side and Stanmer church on the other. The seven bay-fronted house dates back to 1722 and the flint church was built in 1838. Walk across the green, then bear right to cut through the churchyard and go forward onto Stanmer's very pretty street with attractive flint cottages and, at the time of writing, a tea room. Follow the street northwards to its end, then go

Stanmer Park with house and church

straight on along a signed path heading initially just west of north, then northwards, then just east of north, to enter an area of woodland and arrive at a path crossroads. Go straight over, immediately veering left and descending through the woods; you emerge in the valley, then continue on along the obvious path, heading north-eastwards and uphill, round the edge of Bow Hill. At the top you arrive at a gate and signed path junction, here turning hard right along a signed bridleway, enjoying excellent views to Falmer and the Amex Stadium. You descend along the bridleway to reach a path junction just short of St Mary's Farm; go straight on past the farm buildings along a driveway, then rise gently, keeping woodland to the left and soon getting tremendous views to the South Downs and Brighton. Continue on along the road which is now Ridge Road, descending steadily.

At length you reach Mill Street going off to the right; ignore this turn but continue on, turning right with the road. Just before the Swan Inn which is on the right, turn left to climb the steps to cross the footbridge over the A27. Turn left at the end along a narrow path, then veer right along a lane to reach the old village of Falmer with its church, green (including village pump), pond and good views to the downland south of the village. Follow the pond round clockwise past the church of St Laurence; you need to join a lane briefly at the top end, but soon bear right onto a green path which continues beside the pond. Don't go forward to the pump but follow the road at the north-western end of the pond, heading north-west past the Old Post Office, one of a number of lovely flint cottages beside the green and the pond. Veer right to return to the footbridge, crossing back over it.

Now follow the road past the pub round to the right and go up to turn left into Mill Street, following it to another T-junction; go straight over onto a footpath which heads through the trees to reach the Southern Ring Road of the Sussex University campus. Again cross over and continue along the path, which bears left at the fork and descends, crossing a metalled driveway and passing to the right of a redbrick block, meeting the Southern Ring Road once more. Cross over onto a path signed US2, going forward to follow an area of green, continuing as far as a metalled walkway. Join the walkway heading in the same direction and at the junction turn left to walk to the subway you used at the start of the walk, retracing your steps to the station. It's worth climbing up the steps on the south side of the station building to get a good view of the recently built Amex Stadium, the new home of Brighton Football Club and a magnificent piece of modern architecture.

Faygate *(Line A, 4.5 miles, linear walk to Horsham: moderate)*

Walk from the station to the adjacent Faygate Lane and turn right to follow it past

A clearing in St Leonard's Forest

the Holmbush Inn down to a roundabout junction with the A264. Cross carefully on the right side (crossing points are shown) and go straight over to follow Tower Road through the trees for about three quarters of a mile, looking out carefully for a lodge on the left – it's the only building on the left so you shouldn't miss it! – and shortly beyond that, turn right onto a signed path which proceeds south-westwards through the woods to reach Forest Road. Go straight over onto a metalled driveway, and continue south-westwards for about half a mile and arrive at a path junction and clearing, with a seat, information board and superb views. You're now in the heart of St Leonard's Forest, so called because legend says that here St Leonard killed the last dragon in England; the forest once supported a flourishing iron-smelting industry, and mounds called pillow mounds were created to provide accommodation for rabbits who were valued for their fur and as food.

Go straight over the crossroads here, ignoring the path signed left, but almost immediately "your" path veers sharp left and now proceeds southwards in a dead straight line. Half a mile from the clearing you reach a signed path crossroads where you need to turn right along the signed High Weald Landscape Trail (NOT the wide track just short of the finger post). Follow this path through the woods, over a path crossroads, then at a T-junction at Greenbroom Hill, turn right and descend, still through the trees, heading westwards, keeping the pretty stream Sheepwash Gill to the left. You reach the bottom of the hill then climb, emerging from the woods and following the left edge of pasture, reaching a T-junction with a track. Turn left to join the track, going forward onto a signed path, which is narrow but clear, passing through or by the edge of woodland, reaching a T-junction by Stew Pond. Turn right here through woodland, soon arriving at a metalled road, Hamper's Lane, which you follow round to the left, ignoring paths going off to the right.

Keep walking westwards along Hamper's Lane, the surroundings now become more urban, to reach a junction with Comptons Lane. Go pretty much straight over into Depot Road, and follow this past the Millais School for just over half a mile to the end, reaching a T-junction with Station Road. To access the station turn left into Station Road and, as it bends left, bear right and immediately right again to the rear station entrance. There are automatic ticket barriers here; if the barriers are operational and you can't get through them for any reason, you'll need to backtrack down Station Road, going forward to a roundabout and turning hard left into North Street which takes you to the main station entrance. To access Horsham's centre from here, please refer to the Horsham station walk below.

Fishbourne *(Line A, 4.5 miles, circular walk: easy)*

Walk southwards down Salthill Road from the station exit, and turn shortly left into Roman Way. Soon on your right you will arrive at the excellent Fishbourne Roman Palace remains, exhibition and café; there was once a substantial Roman palace here, remaining until the 5th century AD and containing magnificent mosaic floors incorporating floral motifs, dolphins, fish and vases. Having visited the complex, continue along the metalled cycle path/walkway which veers right and heads for the A259, bending sharp left as it reaches the main road. On this bend, go forward to cross straight over the road onto a narrow signed footpath which heads southwards from the A259, soon crossing a stream and reaching a field. Continue along the path across the field aiming for a gate then follow the left-hand field edge to the field corner, reaching a path junction. Go ahead into the next field and take the obvious path heading half-right over the field to reach another field boundary and path junction, proceeding straight on across another field to arrive at the harbourside (1).

Now follow the clear embankment path on the left bank of the harbour waters, describing a semi-circle; if you were in a hurry you could shortly join a path which effects a short cut across. You're then forced slightly away from the waterside along a path through a field, keeping the harbour to your right. Towards the end of the field, with trees immediately ahead, turn left onto another signed path leading away from the harbour, soon entering the churchyard of the pretty 13th century Appledram church. Turn right along the church path which widens into a lane, then at the end turn left onto a road which arrives at a T-junction with Appledram Lane. Your way is right here, but by turning left you'll reach the main entrance to Rymans, a stone built manor house with a tower dating back to 1410. Now proceed down Appledram Lane to a T-junction with Dell Quay Road, turning right to follow this to Dell Quay village and its Crown and Anchor pub, said to be at least 400 years old. Dell Quay was formerly a very busy port and ranked in the 8th century as the most important town in Sussex. It was particularly busy in Elizabethan times, with 3 vessels sailing from here to fight the Armada, was flourishing as a port throughout the 18th century, but following its decline as a port it has found a new prosperity in the form of sailing and boating.

  Pass the pub, turn right onto the harbourside path and now head back towards Fishbourne, enjoying lovely views across the waters and northwards to Kingley Vale; I suggest that beyond the field path which provided the Appledram turning on the way down, you do use the short cut this time to avoid the embankment and reach point (1) then continue alongside the water past its northern end, proceeding along a board walk and arriving at a path T-junction. Turn left here along a clear path which proceeds through the trees by a stream, arriving at the bottom of Mill Lane. Turn right up Mill Lane, keeping the pretty mill pond to your left, soon arriving at the A259 and bearing left to follow it. You shortly reach the junction with Salthill Road, turning right up this road to return to the station.

Fishersgate *(Line B, 5.5 miles, linear walk to Shoreham-by-Sea: moderate)*

Exit Fishersgate station by the footpath heading north-westwards from the east end of the north platform, and walk north-westwards along a dead straight path, going over four road crossings, Manor Hall Road, then the busy A270 Old Shoreham Road (by a garden centre/café), then Mile Oak Road, then Mile Oak Gardens. You arrive at the bottom end of a field, but your signed path proceeds through the trees immediately to the right of the field, continuing in the same north-westerly direction. The path kinks slightly right; another path comes in from the right and you continue briefly beyond that point, but soon veer left to arrive at the field edge. Now simply follow the right-hand field edge on a clear path. You arrive at a footpath junction by a gate and here turn left to follow the signed bridleway, shortly passing under two lines of pylons. You then veer gently right, and go straight ahead along an excellent level path, keeping the pylons to the right. Ignore a path shortly forking right, keeping straight on, rising a little, passing through a thin area of vegetation and going forward to reach a fence with a track behind. There's a finger post here; ignore the path going hard right but bear half-right to walk beside the fence then, on very shortly reaching a gate, go through it and turn right to join the track behind, now on the course of the Monarch's Way and also on Southwick Hill. The fiddly route finding is behind you!

  It's now easy walking on an excellent track which veers left and rises steadily, with great views opening up. You pass a trig point and shortly beyond it go through a gate (1) and veer slightly right, walking uphill; at the top of the rise there's another gate, immediately beyond which leave the path by turning left to the summit of the

Looking down on the Adur valley from Mill Hill

hill, Thunders Barrow. The views from here are quite astonishing, to Brighton in the east, the Isle of Wight to the south-west, the masts of Truleigh Hill to the north-west, and a massive section of coastline including Brighton, Southwick, Shoreham, Worthing and Littlehampton. Retrace your steps to the gate at (1) but this time, having gone through it, veer round to the right and then right again along a clear path heading westwards along the hillside. The views from this path are quite superb until your path goes very steeply downhill. Go forward to Mossy Bottom Barn, picking up a metalled farm lane, following it round to the right and climbing slightly, then veer left and drop to the tree-shaded buildings of Erringham Farm.

Follow the lane past the farm buildings, veering sharply left, then right, then left again to climb to a T-junction, turning left here along Mill Hill. Initially the views are obscured by woodland, but beyond this and a nature reserve car park there's a superb view to the Adur valley including the meandering river Adur, the imposing Lancing College Chapel, and the Shoreham flyover which also has a certain elegance. The views to the coast beyond aren't bad either! The nature reserve boasts many wild flowers and butterflies, including the rare Adonis Blue. Save for an interruption for a reservoir, it's possible here to walk along the grass to the right of Mill Hill road but you need to return to it in order to cross the A27. Beyond the bridge crossing you descend quite steeply to a T-junction with Erringham Road, turning left to follow it to Upper Shoreham Road. Cross straight over into Mill Lane, following this to the lovely partially-flint Sycamore Cottage, turning left just before it to continue along Mill Lane to a T-junction with Buckingham Road. Turn right here, and you'll soon reach Shoreham-by-Sea station on the left.

Ford *(Line A, 2 miles, linear walk to Arundel: easy)*

From the station, turn right and walk down Station Road. In a little over a quarter of a mile you reach Ford Lane on the right; bear left almost opposite this turning onto a signed path leading you towards the very pretty unspoilt Norman church of St Andrew by the Ford. Turn left immediately before the churchyard fence and follow the path round, veering right, then having passed the church, veer gently left with the path and climb onto the bank above the river. At the path junction at the top, bear left to follow a tiny inlet round, very shortly arriving at the river bank. Go forward to pass under the railway then continue to follow the left bank of the river to Arundel. Throughout this walk, there are magnificent views to Arundel, its cathedral and castle.

At length you reach the A27, passing underneath it and going forward to a new riverside development. Bear slightly left here to arrive at Tarrant Street and go straight on along it with its many lovely houses, shops, cafes and restaurants, several of the houses dating back to the 18th century. Highlights include the grand flint-fronted Nineveh Chapel, now converted into antique and craft shops; the white weatherboarded Belindas, a superbly civilised place to enjoy a cream tea; the brick-built Sparks Yard, where a wall inscription shows that Sparks was previously an auctioneer, valuer and appraiser; the yellow-washed Bay Tree restaurant with over-hanging upper storey; and the Old Printing Works, now converted into a parade of little shops. I recommend you turn left up the steep cobbled Kings Arms Hill, turn right into the splendid Maltravers Street, follow it briefly then

One of the lovely buildings in Tarrant Street, Arundel

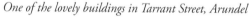

turn right down another cobbled street, Bakers Arms Hill, and left to continue along Tarrant Street. At the end, turn right to walk down to the quay; bear round to the left along the riverside and arrive at the bridge crossing of the Arun. Turn right to walk along Queen Street and arrive at a roundabout junction with the A27. Go straight on, crossing the road at the pedestrian crossing and soon reaching Arundel station to your right.

Frant *(Line H, 4 miles, linear walk to Tunbridge Wells: easy)*

Turn left out of the main station exit to follow the B2169 Bayham Road for just over a mile, mostly uphill; it's quite a busy road but the views especially to your left are good. As you reach the sign advertising you have arrived in Royal Tunbridge Wells, turn right onto the signed High Weald Landscape Trail, passing immediately to the left (north-west) of the Nevill Golf Club, its clubhouse and car park to arrive at a T-junction with Benhall Mill Lane. Turn left to follow it for a few hundred yards, but just before the houses start on the right, turn right onto a signed path which soon veers left, north-westwards, in the shade of trees. You arrive at a junction with Forest Road, turning left then immediately right into Warwick Park, with an excellent view ahead to Tunbridge Wells. Now follow Warwick Park downhill, and shortly after veering right with the road, turn left along Roedean Road, right at the T-junction into Frant Road and left into Montacute Road. You pass over the course of the defunct Tunbridge Wells-Tunbridge Wells West railway, and then bear left into Linden Park Road past the old Tunbridge Wells West station, magnificently restored, and across a roundabout by a superstore to reach the "new" Tunbridge Wells West station, the headquarters of the Spa Valley Railway (see Eridge walk).

Retrace your steps briefly to the roundabout but now turn left to immediately reach a roundabout junction with the A26 Eridge Road/London Road. Turn right to follow it but shortly bear right again at the bottom of Linden Park Road at Union Square, and immediately left to arrive at the Pantiles. This is a pedestrian precinct laid down in the 18th century lined by trees and colonnades of 18th and 19th century houses and shops, and some buildings dating back as far as the 17th century; the heyday of the Pantiles was in the 18th century when Beau Nash was a frequent visitor. I suggest you follow the middle row of houses/shops first, past the bandstand, then on reaching the chalybeate spring – recognised centuries ago as the source of health-giving waters which helped to establish Tunbridge Wells as a popular resort – walk back along the north-western most row (left-hand side looking from the bottom end). Lastly follow the right-hand row including the elegant Corn Exchange shopping mall; at the Tourist Information booth turn left and then right to follow the middle of the Pantiles to its end, veering right and then right again to cross Nevill Street using the pedestrian crossing. Turn left beyond the crossing, right and then left up Chapel Place, but it's worth detouring to the end of Nevill Street to visit the church of King Charles the Martyr which dates back to 1678 and boasts a white marble font, impressive wooden cupola, galleries and plaster ceiling.

Walk up Chapel Place and go straight on into the High Street with its elegant

The elegant Pantiles in Tunbridge Wells

independent shops, continuing on along the right hand side, crossing the railway and Grove Hill Road to reach the magnificent Great Hall Arcade. Immediately beyond it turn right and follow a road to enter Calverley Grounds, shortly before forking left. Continue very pleasantly through the grounds along the path, veering left to pass the near side of the basketball court, then at the top carry straight on to arrive at a junction of driveways. Turn left here to aim for an archway but just before it look to the right at the splendid Calverley Park Crescent, part of an estate designed by the great architect Decimus Burton.

Carry on through the archway, turning left to follow Crescent Road downhill to just short of a very busy crossroads. Turn right here to cross over Crescent Road and walk up the steps to follow Civic Way, parallel with Mount Pleasant Road, past the Georgian-style Town Hall and the town's museum and art gallery. Then return to Mount Pleasant Road, admiring the green-domed redbrick former opera house on the right, then at a zebra crossing just before a slight left bend in the main thoroughfare, bear left to a fork junction. Take the right fork, Mount Ephraim Road, heading uphill. As you reach a green, turn half left along a path signed "The Common," soon crossing London Road and going forward to a T-junction with the A264 Mount Ephraim. Turn left to follow beside this road, observing the excellent Royal Wells Hotel which is to the right, the vegetation clearing to allow a superb view across the town and beyond. Shortly beyond an information board by the pavement, bear left onto a footpath forking away from the road, crossing over a gravelled drive to immediately reach a crossroads of paths. Turn left here and walk steeply down to cross just to the left of a very busy road junction, going straight on into Church Road. Before proceeding, look back up the hillside to observe the rocky outcrops straight ahead and to the right, then look across Church Road at the splendid Jordan House which dates back to 1685. From here follow Church Road eastwards past the old Holy Trinity Church, another of

Burton's designs, now a flourishing arts centre, to reach another busy crossroads. Turn right into Mount Pleasant Road and follow it very steeply downhill; the station is towards the bottom of the hill on the right.

Gatwick Airport *(Lines A & E, 3 miles, circular walk: easy)*

From the platform levels, walk to the main station concourse with railway ticket office and departure boards, and leave the concourse as signed LIFTS FOR PLATFORMS 3-6/EXIT/AIRPORT TERMINALS. Follow the corridor to shortly reach another concourse, part of the airport's South Terminal, with International Arrivals board; on reaching this concourse turn sharp left, passing a Bureau de Change which is to your left, and then bear immediately left again to follow a long passageway, with a parallel conveyor belt, to its end. Turn half-right, going diagonally forward to cross a zebra crossing of a road, then bear right along a corridor which you follow for about 150-200 yards until on your right you go through a door to descend a signed flight of stairs to level G. Go through another door and turn right, soon reaching and walking up a short slipway, going straight on over a small grassy area and across a road to reach a walkway. Turn left to follow the walkway under the flyover, passing Eastway which is to your left, and 200 yards or so beyond Eastway, turn right into Buckingham Gate. The road soon swings left and shortly beyond the bend you turn right as signed for Schlumberger House.

A little beyond Schlumberger House the road bends right by a gate, and just beyond this bend, bear left along a path which takes you to the B2036. Turn right to follow it briefly, then left along Fernhill to a T-junction, turning right here onto Peeks Brook Lane, now on the Sussex Border Path. The lane shortly kinks right, and just beyond here you take the next left turn, Church Lane, crossing the M23 and continuing through a semi-rural landscape with rough vegetation and buildings on both sides. When the tarmac road veers right, carry straight on north-eastwards along a path, which follows a very pleasant course through woodland. You pass to the left of a lovely lake and arrive at Church Road, turning right to walk along Church

The spire of Burstow church

Road through Burstow, a delightful village; of particular note on the right-hand side is the Coach House, with a most unusual post box just outside it, and the splendid redbrick Manor House. However the village's main glory is its church, which has Anglo-Saxon and Norman origins. The bell tower is a rare timber structure with large beams from oaks in Worth Forest and elm cladding, and the oldest of the six bells dates from 1450. The church is best known for its association with John Flamsteed, the first Astronomer Royal in 1675; he was rector of Burstow from 1684 until his death in 1719, he is buried below the chancel, and he is commemorated by, appropriately enough, a star set in the large memorial window above the Altar.

Follow the road to the bottom of the street. As it bends left, bear right onto a driveway and follow it; there is a particularly fine view of the church spire from here. Beyond the buildings your path veers very slightly left, fractionally south of west, and goes forward to cross a footbridge then bears half-right across the pasture to another footbridge and a signed path junction. Go straight ahead along the left-hand field edge, veering slightly right to cross a stile and arrive back at Church Lane. Turn left to follow it back over the M23 to the junction with Peeks Brook Lane and now retrace your steps to Gatwick exactly the way you came, back to the South Terminal complex, with its many refreshment opportunities. Signposting back to the station is excellent if you lose the original route!

Glynde *(Line C, 3 miles, circular walk: moderate)*

From the station walk up to the road and head northwards, across Glynde Reach to the attractive village centre. Turn shortly left into Ranscombe Lane, passing the village shop which is to your left, and a very short way beyond the shop, to your right, go through a gate onto a signed path heading north-westwards. You strike out across a field, veering gently left, and, keeping a fence immediately to the left, ascend steadily; go forward over a stile and then continue uphill, heading for the shoulder of Mount Caburn which is the hilltop to your half-left ahead. At length the ground levels out, giving a great view towards Lewes. You dip very slightly and immediately before a stile in the fence (1) turn left along a clear field-edge path then rise across springy grass to the summit of Mount Caburn. There are superb views to the South Downs escarpment and the Ouse valley, and across a vast expanse of more level East Sussex countryside. Retrace your steps to (1) but now continue beside the fence slightly uphill to a post (2), turning right here onto a permissive path which drops to a gate and stile and then passes through trees, emerging to give a fabulous view eastwards to Firle Beacon and Windover Hill. Continue on down the path kinking right then left at the bottom to turn right onto Lacy's Hill.

Descend past Glynde Place, a magnificent flint-built Elizabethan house, and then the 18th century parish church, also of flint, both on the left. Carry on downhill past the end of Ranscombe Lane and simply retrace your steps to the station. Note that if permission to walk the permissive path

The superb view towards Firle Beacon from below Mount Caburn

starting at (2) is withdrawn you'll need to retrace your steps from (2) to (1) and then bear left to walk back to Glynde the way you came up. To visit Glynde Church and Glynde Place, detour left up Lacy's Hill from the end of Ranscombe Lane before returning to the station. If you fancy a drink before your train home, the Trevor Arms is a short way beyond the station on the right.

Goring-by-Sea *(Line B, 3 miles, circular walk: moderate)*

From the north side of the station walk up Goring Street (a walkway cuts a corner), bearing left at a junction with the A259 along footpath/cycle path to a roundabout. Go straight over up Titnore Lane for just over a quarter of a mile, turning left onto a signed public byway which approaches some buildings; follow the signed path immediately to the right of the buildings, then rise gently, following the right-hand side of the open space, and ascend onto Highdown Hill. You pass well to the right of the so-called Miller's Tomb, the tomb of the 18th century eccentric John Olliver, and continue uphill, avoiding paths going off to the left. As you near the summit of Highdown Hill, you arrive at a signed junction of paths; aim now for the earthwork which you can see ahead, and follow the path in the shade of trees, passing the earthwork, detouring, if you wish, to the trig point, now on the highest ground of Highdown Hill. The views are magnificent, with the tops of the South Downs clearly visible to the north, and on a clear day you can see the Isle of Wight, Selsey Bill, Chichester Cathedral and even Beachy Head. The earthwork is the site of a hillfort which dates back to the Iron Age and which was re-fortified in the 3rd century AD, and there's also a pagan Saxon cemetery within the ramparts.

Continue along the path, soon reaching a junction, turning (very!) hard left, here and walking downhill, passing just to the right of the Olliver memorial and dropping down to a car park. Immediately to the right is the entrance to the chalk gardens, which are free to enter and well worth a visit, particularly in spring when the colours are at their most majestic; next door is the Highdown Hotel with restaurant and tea room. From here follow the road downhill, then at a sign on the right prohibiting horse-riding, turn right to follow the left side of playing fields, descending and enjoying good views ahead. On reaching the parking area, turn left to return to the road and right again along the road to arrive at the A259. Cross straight over and turn left along the cyclepath/walkway, arriving back at the roundabout; turn right and then shortly right again alongside Goring Street to return to the station.

Hampden Park *(Line C, 2 miles, circular walk: easy)*

From the station walk to the main street, turning left past the parade of shops, and forward along Brassey Avenue. The road bends sharp left and becomes Nevill Avenue, then bends sharp right, becoming Decoy Drive. Almost immediately on the right beyond the right bend is the striking church of St Mary; opposite the church bear left along a narrow path which enters the trees of Hampden Park itself. Previously owned by Lord Willingdon, this was the first Corporation-owned park in Eastbourne, opened by Lord Rosebery in August 1902. Having entered the trees, turn right at the first main path junction and follow the path through woods which are a mixture of oak, ash, field maple and beech. At the path T-junction at the end, turn right, then left at the next major path junction (1) just before Decoy Drive. Follow the path to a T-junction with Hampden Park Drive, turning left and following the drive until you reach the lake. Turn left to follow the left-hand edge of the lake briefly, then right over the little footbridge (2) signed for the café, then beyond the footbridge, veer left to walk beside the lake, with a the café to the right.

At the top corner of the lake, veer left then right to describe a semi-circle round very attractive gardens with splendid displays of crocuses, daffodils and bluebells in spring, palm and monkey puzzle trees, and mini-waterfalls. Return to the lakeside path and follow it round to the footbridge at (2) above, going forward to Hampden Park Drive (there is a lovely stretch of water in view on the other side of the drive too). Bear right and then right again to retrace your steps to (1) again but this time go forward along a path through the trees which veers right to reach a path T-junction. Turn left here, then left at the next major path junction along a path which returns you to Decoy Drive with St Mary's Church opposite. Bear right to retrace your steps back to the station.

Hassocks *(Line E, 6 miles, circular walk: strenuous)*

Leave the station by the down platform exit and walk briefly down the station approach road; opposite the pub turn right down steps to meet the main street (B2116) which you cross, turn right and walk towards the railway bridge. Just before it, take the second of two signed paths going left, running parallel with and just to the left of the railway for about a mile, ending by the T-junction of the B2112, coming in from the left, with the A273. Walk very briefly up the A273 then turn left into Underhill Lane, soon reaching the church of St John the Baptist which boasts a pre-1066 chancel arch and superb medieval wall paintings dating from 1140. Continue down Underhill Lane briefly then turn right up a bridleway signed South Downs Way (SDW), and keep to the obvious signed (blue arrow) bridleway, rapidly gaining height and looking back to enjoy magnificent views. You now approach the two windmills, Jack and Jill, to your right, and aim for the clear path skirting the left (north-east) side of the mills. Jill, the right-hand one as you look at them, is undoubtedly the more attractive and photogenic with its sails and bright white colour; the darker Jack, to the left, is something of a poor relation, lacking any sails! To visit Jill, open to visitors at certain times, detour right and walk through the car park to reach the entrance gate, then return to the path the same way.

Beyond the mills, keep along the path uphill, arriving at a T-junction where you turn left onto a clear track heading south-eastwards. Very shortly the SDW comes in from the right, and you now follow it all the way to Ditchling Beacon, initially continuing to climb, keeping the fence to your left. You then veer gently left, from south-eastwards to just north of east, arriving at and following the top of the scarp, passing just to the right of clumps of bushes and one of the characteristic dewponds of the SDW; you shortly pass to the left of another dewpond, then begin a very clear and quite stiff climb, signalling your approach to the climax of the walk. As you climb, you keep a fence to your right. The fence bends sharply to the right and immediately beyond this bend, walk to the Ditchling Beacon trig point above you to

Looking west from Ditchling Beacon

the right; from the trig point there's a tremendous panorama, stretching across the Downs for miles in both directions, the Weald to the north, and the sea to the south. Make your way back to the SDW and just continue a little further east to enjoy a superb view to Blackcap, the next big summit on the South Downs.

Now you head back towards Hassocks along the SDW, initially downhill then along the top of the escarpment, rising very steadily to the wooden signpost known as Keymer Post, roughly a mile from Ditchling Beacon. Turn right here onto the signed bridleway which heads steeply downhill, then in roughly half a mile veers right. At this point, fork left onto a signed path which descends through the trees to reach Underhill Lane, going straight over to follow a grassy path which veers to the right, keeping an attractive lake to the right. Follow the signed path through the meadow, then as the lake veers away to the right and you get within sight of the eastern end of the meadow, veer round to the left and walk up to a gate at the top end, beyond which you go forward to arrive at Lodge Lane. Turn left to follow it down to the B2112 New Road, crossing straight over and following it, passing a particularly fine thatched and timbered cottage and arriving at the B2116 in the centre of Keymer. Turn left to follow the road back to Hassocks with its good range of shops and cafes, bearing right along the approach road to arrive at the station.

Hastings *(Lines C & H, 2.5 miles, circular walk: easy)*

Go straight ahead out of the station exit down Havelock Road to the central shopping precinct; bear left past McDonald's, passing under Albert Road using a pedestrian underpass, and reaching a roundabout junction with the coast road. Follow the coast road on, sticking to the inland side, shortly forking left into the fascinating George Street with its independent shops and stunning pub, Ye Olde Pumphouse. At the end turn right then almost immediately left along East Street, passing the Royal Standard Inn; arrive at and cross straight the coast road over into Rock-a-Nore Road, noting the modern Jerwood Gallery with its displays of 20th century art, including works by Lowry and Augustus John, to the right. Shortly you need to bear left up the Tamarisk Steps, just before the Dolphin Inn, but you should detour along Rock-a-Nore Road with its fishermen's huts and fish shops, to visit the Fishermen's Museum and just beyond, the Shipwreck Museum.

Climb Tamarisk Steps, following the sign for East Hill, and turn sharp left to follow Tackleway, admiring East Hill House, sometime home of HRH Duke of Sussex; enjoy the lovely view to Hastings down Oxford Terrace, and also the impressive Trafalgar Cottages, Woods Passage, the weatherboarded Strawberry Cottage and the redbrick Tackleway Hall. At the end of Tackleway turn left into the churchyard of All Saints Church, and walk along the path through the churchyard; if the church is open it's worth visiting, with its particularly striking wall-painting depicting Christ in judgment. Exit the churchyard via the steps and turn left down All Saints Street, with several quaint and attractive cottages, arguably the best being the timber-framed Shovells, home of the mother of a 17th century admiral, splendidly named Cloudesley Shovell. Your continuous route bears right down an alley just before no 121, but it's worth detouring on down All Saints Street as far as the superb timber-framed no 58 and 59, returning and then following the alley as stated to reach the Bourne. Turn right up the Bourne, passing the superb flint-built RC church of St Mary Star Of The Sea which

A 15th century gem in All Saints Street

is to the left, then take the next turning left, keeping the splendid Old Hastings House immediately to the right, and turn left again into the High Street.

Walk down the High Street, noting the amusingly-named pub First In Last Out to your left, and the lovely timber-framed Nos 102 and 103 opposite, two of a number of fine half-timbered houses in the street. You pass a quaint toy shop, Upfield & Sons, some art galleries, the Electric Palace Cinema, and the lovely Old Town Maritime Garden, created in 2008. Pass the tempting Judges Bakery, and turn right into Swan Terrace to arrive at Hastings' other surviving medieval church, St Clement's; Hill Street going off Swan Terrace to the left contains the lovely timber-framed Swan Hotel. Bear round to the right into Croft Road, then bear right down Church Passage to return to the High Street. (Before going down Church Passage it's worth detouring up Croft Road to see the superb timber-framed number 49.) Turn right to return to Judges, repeat your walk up Swan Terrace, but this time go straight up Coburg Place, signed for the castle and caves. Veer left and pass through a "tunnel," turning right to climb onto the green, now on West Hill. Having reached the green, walk to your right aiming for a white-painted building resembling a lighthouse, and you'll reach the entrance to St Clement's Caves, a network of sandstone underground tunnels providing graphic and interactive exhibitions devoted to smuggling. From here, bear hard left to make your way south-westwards across the grass to the highest point of West Hill, providing superb views to the town and the sea. Then follow the obvious path down to the castle entrance; built shortly after the Norman invasion, with the keep being built by Henry II in 1172, most of it has now been washed away by the sea. Now follow the main castle approach road away from the entrance gate then turn left into Castle Hill Road; at the T-junction at the bottom turn left and cross the road, then bear shortly right and immediately left into the elegant Wellington Square. Follow the left side of the square down and aim for McDonald's ahead, then having reached McDonald's bear right through the central shopping area, and walk back up Havelock Road to return to the station.

Haywards Heath *(Line E, 4.5 miles, circular walk: easy)*

Cross straight over the road in front of the station and turn right to immediately reach a roundabout, turning left here into Mill Green Road; follow it to its end, turning right into College Road and almost immediately left into Wickham Way. At the end turn right and walk past Wickham Farm, soon reaching a signed path junction with paths going straight on and left. Turn left to head northwards along a well defined path in the shade of trees, emerging at a golf course; follow the finger posts, veering just east of north and continuing to rise gently in pretty much a straight line. At the edge of woodland, about three quarters of a mile from Wickham Farm, turn right at a T-junction with the Ouse Valley Way (OVW) and follow the directions on the finger posts across the golf course, veering right then left. The

A delightful corner of Lindfield

going then gets clearer as you go forward just south of east onto a drive that brings you to High Beech Lane. Turn left to follow it downhill, bending left then right, and after a few hundred yards turn right as OVW-signed, down the Kenwards Farm lane. In less than 200 yards turn right onto a rough track, going uphill, keeping the farm to the left and views to the Ouse valley beyond. You reach a junction of tracks and turn left, sticking to the main track, and dropping down into woodland. You then rise again, reaching a further path junction where you turn left on to an enclosed footpath, with houses and gardens to your right and extensive views to the Ouse valley to your left. You arrive in a gravelled courtyard in which you bear right, then shortly left to arrive at the main street at Lindfield, close to the 14th century parish church of St John the Baptist. Your way is to the right, down the B2028 into the village centre, but you will surely want to explore the church and its surroundings first. Just north of the church is the superb 16th century timber-framed Old Place screened from the main street by the 15th century Thatched Cottage, and adjacent is the fine early 18th century redbrick Lindfield House. Proceeding from the church downhill you'll see many lovely houses along the main street, arguably the best being the timber-framed Tiger by the church, the astonishing 15th/16th century timber-framed Barnlands, the Early Georgian redbrick Malling Priory opposite, and, next to Barnlands, the excellent brick-built Nash House. At the bottom of the village is its lovely pond.

Having enjoyed the village and its amenities, leave it by turning right (as you look downhill on the village street) onto Hickmans Lane. As you reach the green on your left, turn left to follow the left-hand edge of the green round, then turn left again to follow a metalled pathway, emerging and skirting the end of a cul-de-sac, going forward to another alleyway which brings you back to Hickmans Lane. Cross straight over along Sunte Avenue, passing the 1845 Witch Inn (noting its "Good Stabling" sign on an outbuilding!) then cross Portsmouth Lane into Gander Hill, ascending then descending and going forward into College Lane. Just before the railway embankment turn left into Mill Green Road which brings you back to the roundabout immediately beyond which is the station.

Horsham *(Line A, 2 miles, circular walk: easy)*

Turn left out of the station exit to follow North Street, passing the splendid timber-framed 17th century North Chapel. Cross at the pedestrian crossing and continue down North Street, forking right into Chart Way and passing the Jubilee Fountain, erected for Queen Victoria's Jubilee in 1897, and the adjacent Bottings, a timber-framed hall house. Continue along Chart Way, past the very impressive Sun Alliance atrium, a glass-clad structure with fine window decoration depicting Sussex scenes, and a magnificent chandelier inside. Go on past the spire of St Mark's Church which stood till recently on this site; the church was built in 1840, the spire being added in 1870 and preserved when the rest of the building was demolished.

One of many beautiful buildings in Horsham's Causeway

Descend to Carfax, turning left to pass the front of Waitrose and turn left into Pirie's Alley, a medieval twitten, passing the timber-framed Pirie's Bar and going forward to Pirie's Place, noting a fine bronze statue of Mr Pirie, a former local headmaster, and his donkey.

Return to Carfax and turn left to continue, soon passing the Ask Italian restaurant labelled AD 1401, the lettering on the wall indicating that this was once an Inland Revenue office. Go straight on to the Old Town Hall which looks like a castle – it was built by the Duke of Norfolk in 1812 on the site of the former Market House – and pass round its left side, now on Market Square. Easily missed but well worth detouring down is Talbot Lane or Pump Alley, another narrow twitten at the entrance to which is the Old Posting Box, an early collection point for London mail. There are some fine timber-framed buildings down this twitten. Return to the market square and turn left, going into the Causeway, arguably the finest street in Horsham. You pass the town museum, with excellent information office, and keeping the fine Manor House (built on the site of Hewells, a 12th century manor) to the right, continue southwards along the Causeway past some really excellent buildings to the left including the stunning pink timber-framed no 12. There's another lovely alley, Morth Gardens, just beyond, while a plaque on number 18 shows the author Hammond Innes lived here between 1919 and 1924.

At the end of the Causeway is the mainly 13th century St Mary's Church, boasting a towering shingled spire; note the lovely Sylvan Mews, dating from 1615, on the right just before the church. Pass round the right-hand side of the church and walk on southwards along the path past the lovely Remembrance Garden, then just before the bridge over the infant river Arun turn right to enjoy a lovely riverside walk, shortly passing the 19th century Provender Mill. Soon you arrive at a junction, turning right onto the busy Worthing Road, going straight over a roundabout by Sainsbury's, shortly passing the fine 1786 Quakers' Meeting House and the lovely Unitarian Church, built as a Baptist church in 1721 and set in lovely gardens. Go forward to the pedestrianized Bishopric and the striking water sculpture, Rising Universe, completed in 1966 to mark Horsham's connection with the poet Shelley who was born just outside the town.

At the fountain turn right into West Street, Horsham's main shopping thoroughfare, and follow it to Waterstones; immediately beyond it turn left to follow Carfax, the centuries-old centre of the town with its cobbles and gas lamps as well as war memorial and bandstand. Fairs and markets have been held in this area since the 13th century, and there are some fine timber-framed buildings dating from the 15th to 17th centuries. At the top end aim just to the left of Waitrose to rejoin Chart Way and go forward up North Street towards the station, passing Park House which is to your left, built between 1690 and 1720. Continuing on the left-hand side of North Street, you pass a group of lovely 17th century cottages also to your left, the first cottage, white and weatherboarded, particularly charming. From here, continue to the roundabout, crossing over to return to the station.

Hove *(Line B, 3 miles, circular walk: easy)*

Turn left out of the station forecourt along Station Approach, soon bearing right and then left, turning right down Eaton Gardens. You turn left at the T-junction with Eaton Road to follow it to the crossroads junction with the Drive, going straight over and past the church of All Saints, Hove's grandest Anglican church, built of Horsham sandstone in 1890-1891. There's a fine red brick house just beyond. Continue along Eaton Road and at the end turn right into Palmeira Avenue, following it seawards, passing the sometime home of the cricketer Jack Hobbs. Turn right into Church Road, crossing to the church of St John the Baptist, then bear left along Western Road and right into Palmeira Square, lovely gardens between two very impressive lines of 19th century houses. Go straight down to reach the even more splendid Adelaide Crescent, designed by the well-known architect Decimus Burton; turn left to follow the crescent round to the bottom, then left again, dropping down to the coast road. Stay on the "land" side to walk along the parallel Brunswick Terrace, soon reaching Brunswick Square, perhaps Hove's finest square with its magnificent brown stone houses, built in the 1820s, around a green. Turn left to walk up the green, exiting it at the top and turning right into Western Road, but very shortly turn right into Brunswick Street East and follow it seawards. Just before the Conqueror pub turn left; don't turn right into Lower Market Street but carry straight on, veering left then right to reach Waterloo Street. On your way you pass firstly the delectable little Old Market Theatre and then the recently restored Waterloo Arch.

Turn right to follow Waterloo Street, passing the stunning Victorian church of St

The sad remains of Brighton's West Pier

Andrew which is to the left (visiting times very limited). Continue on to the coast road, crossing over and bearing left, following the upper promenade to see the splendid Victorian bandstand near the ruined skeleton of the old West Pier. Retrace your steps briefly, then join the seafront promenade and follow it westwards past Brunswick Square and Adelaide Crescent. As you approach the buildings of King's Esplanade, the first incursion of buildings onto the "coastal" side of the main coast road, detour to the imposing statue of Queen Victoria at the end of Grand Avenue. Continue on to the King's Esplanade, turn shortly right through the park on Medina Terrace, then cross straight over the coast road, Kingsway, noting the fine Courtenay House, sometime home of actress Elizabeth Allan, to the right, and the green-domed Alibi pub down the street to the left. Go on up the impressive Medina Villas, turning left at the end into Church Road; go straight over Hove Street into New Church Road, soon reaching Hove Museum and Art Gallery which is to your right. It contains many works by such famous artists as Constable, Hogarth and Gainsborough and superb contemporary crafts and decorative arts collections. Note also the fine Jaipur Gateway in the grounds, built for the Colonial Exhibition of 1886. Return along Church Road passing St Andrew's Old Church, several good shops and restaurants, then just before the modern Town Hall turn left up Norton Road past the fine Catholic Church. At the end turn left, then turn second right up Goldstone Villas to return to the station.

Ifield *(Line A, 3 miles, circular walk: easy)*

From the up platform exit follow Ifield Drive briefly northwards then turn very shortly left down Tangmere Road and right along Rusper Road. Just beyond Oakside turn left at the distinctive yellow entrance to the Rusper Road playing field but actually before the entrance turn immediately right along a thin permissive footpath through rough grass, soon turning right at a T-junction with a wider path. Continue very roughly parallel with Rusper Road northwards, the path becoming a proper signed footpath through rough grass and heading for Ifield church. (Should the permissive path become unavailable, simply follow Rusper Road on to the signed footpath just beyond the house Cotswold, turning left then right as signed onto the northward path.) Go straight on along the right-hand edge of the rough grass with houses to the right, and over a stile into the churchyard. Keep straight on through the churchyard to reach the main church path; by detouring right here you'll reach a road soon bringing you to the popular Plough Inn and a lovely adjoining tile-hung cottage. Then make your way into the church. Dating back to the 13th and 14th centuries, its most notable features are the two 14th century life-size effigies depicting Sir John de Ifelde and Lady Margaret de Ifelde, their feet on lions and their heads supported by angels. Come out of the church and bear left, walking across the churchyard to exit it by the metalled gate at the south-west corner. Now head along an obvious path just south of west, soon reaching a path junction, taking the right-hand path and crossing Ifield Brook.

Continue in the same direction to the hamlet of Lower Barn and the pretty Pound Cottages, turning left at a T-junction into Rusper Road, and following it until a very sharp left bend. Bear right here along a signed narrow path, shortly turning hard left at another path junction, soon arriving at a golf course and following the line shown by the finger post out onto the course, aiming just to the right of a clump of fir trees. Immediately beyond the trees, turn sharp left and the now clear path aims just left of the clubhouse; go forward onto the clubhouse approach road, returning to Rusper Road and turning right. You reach another sharp left bend, turning right onto a signed path up Whitehall Drive, going straight on into Peverel Road and descending. Continue along Peverel Road through a housing estate and rise, veering gently left then turning right at a T-junction onto Hyde Drive, and almost immediately reaching a pond to the right. Opposite the pond turn left down Berrymeade Walk, crossing over the railway and reaching a bridge over water. Cross over and bear right into the Bewbush Water Garden, and now follow a path alongside the lake, keeping it to your right; when I visited I was treated to the sight of a duck protecting a veritable army of ducklings on the water's edge! Keep going until the lake narrows to the right, bearing right to cross a bridge, then turn right onto a bridleway with houses to your left, and keeping the lake to your right, return to the road. Turn left to cross back over the railway, then immediately turn right along a signed bridleway. When it veers left, continue along a grass path in the same direction, soon arriving at the Ifield Mill Pond, a lovely haven for wildlife and plant life: look out for the great crested grebe, coot, mallard or dragonfly, and in the water there may be frogs and crayfish, while trees and plants in and

around the water may include willow, alder, yellowflag, reedmace, water mint and yellow iris. Ahead of you is the fine Ifield Mill, built in 1817, and although it closed in 1927, it's been restored and is occasionally open to the public. The pond was a man-made hammer pond constructed for a forge which once stood

The pond and mill at Ifield, now a suburb of Crawley

here. Go forward alongside the pond towards the mill, soon being reunited with the bridleway. Cross over the water by an active waterfall, then immediately turn left (to visit the mill, go straight on) along a lovely little waterside path which then veers right to reach a metalled drive. Turn left to follow the drive to a T-junction with Hyde Drive, bearing right to follow it and soon arriving at a T-junction with Rusper Road. Bear right and follow Rusper Road briefly, shortly bearing right into Tangmere Road, at the end of which turn right to arrive back at Ifield station.

Lancing *(Line B, 6 miles, linear walk to Shoreham-by-Sea: moderate)*

From the station follow South Street seawards, veering left to reach a T-junction by the Farmers pub. Turn right onto what is a continuation of South Street and follow it to a mini-roundabout junction with the A259 Brighton Road. Bear right to follow it very briefly, then cross at the pedestrian crossing and follow the A259 for another few yards, turning left along a signed footpath which takes you to the seafront promenade, an excellent concrete footpath/cycleway. Turn left to follow it eastwards, your view to the sea being impeded by a line of beach huts for a while so you may prefer the shingle. Eventually the huts end and you can follow the concrete path, getting good views to the Downs and Lancing College Chapel to the left; immediately to the left, however, is the Widewater Lagoon, created when a southern shingle bank developed through a combination of storms and longshore drift. It's now a fine nature reserve with plants including sea anemone, sea campion, sea kale, sea thrift and vipers bugloss, and birds including redshank, pied wagtail, black-headed gull, swan, mallard, ringed plover, grey heron and kestrel. Continue alongside the lagoon, in due course reaching further beach huts, so rejoin the shingle here, noting that the lagoon has ended on your left, and the walkway is now an ordinary coast road. You pass (perhaps visit) the picturesque Church of the Good Shepherd then continue along the shingle bank, which you now follow all the way to West Breakwater, the wall marking the western border of the mouth of the river Adur. Plan to do the walk at low tide when you can follow the softer sand at the bottom of the shingle bank! At the far end of the shingle, clamber to the top of the bank of the Adur, walking to the end of the breakwater to get tremendous views inland and along a huge section of coastline. Then walk briefly beside the Adur estuary along the left bank, almost immediately reaching the brick-built Shoreham Fort, probably Napoleonic in origin but finished in 1857; it was rendered obsolete in 1870 by developments in artillery, although guns remained in situ here till 1921.

Walk round past the fort, keeping it to your left, and through the fort car park to follow a road, Fort Haven, to a T-junction and turn right onto Harbour Road. Just beyond a road going off to the right, turn right (1) onto an unsigned path which shortly brings you back to the riverside and you then follow it; Harbour Road soon comes in and runs parallel with you to your left, and indeed if the path from point (1) became unavailable, you could just stick to Harbour Road throughout, leaving the roadside to continue beside the river. You soon reach the conspicuously signed Quay Court and beside it there's a signed footpath which goes to the right of the buildings and arrives below a fence separating you from a concrete walkway at right-angles. Turn left to follow the fence, soon reaching a gap and going through it to join the walkway, Osprey Way, turning right to follow it to the riverside. Simply veer left to follow what is an excellent waterfront waterway, keeping the impressive new houses and flats to your left; there's an inlet where you need to follow the walkway round, but you're soon back by the river and keep beside it till you're

The church of St Mary de Haura

forced back to the road. Turn right to walk beside the road, then just beyond the Waterside Inn bear right again, and on reaching the waterfront, veer left to follow the riverside briefly, soon arriving at the Dolphin Footbridge, opened in 1921 to replace a ferry crossing.* Having crossed, go straight over the A259 into East Street, now in the heart of Shoreham-by-Sea. (At the time of writing the bridge was being rebuilt; if it hasn't reopened when you visit, continue along the waterfront on a good footpath keeping housing to the left and boats to the right; at the end of the path bear right to cross the road bridge, then continue on along the main shopping street to reach the Shoreham side of the bridge, turning left into East Street.) Follow East Street to a T-junction with St Mary's Road, turning right and then shortly left into Brunswick Road, soon reaching Shoreham-by-Sea station on the right.

Lewes *(Lines C & F, 2.5 miles, circular walk: easy)*

Using the main station exit, cross Station Road and turn left to a junction, bearing right to follow Priory Street to a mini-roundabout; continue straight on along Southover High Street to the magnificent timber-framed Anne of Cleves House, an early 16th century Wealden hall house, now an excellent museum. As you approach the house, you should detour left firstly to the Norman church of St John, and then down Cockshut Road, passing under the railway and turning left to visit the imposing ruins of the Cluniac 11th century priory of St Pancras. Return to the mini-roundabout and turn left. You pass the Kings Head pub then go past a line of splendid colourful old cottages to the very pretty Grange Gardens which are to your right, while to your left is St James Hospital, a lovely flint-fronted building founded in Norman times to provide hospitality for pilgrims as well as the sick. Beyond the gardens is Southover Grange itself, a magnificent 16th century building of Caen stone and the sometime home of the diarist John Evelyn. Continue up the delightful cobbled Keere Street, highlights being the brick built Caprons with lovely garden, the white-painted no 14, the

Beautiful Keere Street, arguably the prettiest street in Lewes

brick-built no 17 and the fine flint no 25. The best is saved till last, the superb timber-framed Fifteenth Century Bookshop at the top end on the left.

Turn right onto the High Street, shortly on the right passing Bull House, built in 1450 and between 1768 and 1774 the home of Thomas Paine, author of *Rights Of Man*. On the left is the historic church of St Michael, boasting a twisting needle spire and 13th century tower, with the fine flint-built Church House immediately adjacent, and the very photogenic clock immediately above. Continue along the High Street then turn shortly left into the Castle Precinct, although you should look across the road at no 74, a superb timber-framed house with the date 1330 inscribed on its wall. Having turned left into Castle Precint you'll reach the ruins of the castle, Norman in origin, although the superb outer gatehouse (Barbican) was added in the 14th century, and enjoy tremendous views from the towers. Then continue along the road through the castle grounds with several notable houses including the Barbican with 17th century interior, and the very splendid Castlegate House beyond which is a green which was first used for bowling in 1640. You arrive at a delightful viewpoint with seats, where the road veers right; here turn left into Castle Banks, but pause to enjoy the superb brick-built tile-hung house on the corner. Walk down Castle Banks to Mount Pleasant, going straight over down Abinger Place, bearing left then immediately right down St John's Hill past the church of St John sub Castro. Cross over Pelham Terrace and go forward along a lovely path next to a strip of water, a delightful area of Lewes known as the Pells.

Return to the bottom of Abinger Place, turning left into Lancaster Street then shortly right up St John's Street and left along West Street; cross the car park on the right and enter the Old Needlemakers, previously a Victorian industrial building and now a superb complex of shops including an excellent bookshop and café. Emerge and turn right along Market Street (if the complex is closed, enter the street round its top end). Turn right into the High Street, passing the imposing town hall which is on the right-hand side, and crossing Fisher Street, very shortly crossing High Street to reach the splendid Georgian White Hart. Turn left into St Andrew's Lane, passing the 16th century Pelham House, one of Lewes' finest buildings, then at the bottom turn left and go forward to a crossroads, here bearing right to reach the station.

Littlehampton *(Line B, 2.5 miles, circular walk: easy)*

Go straight out of the station over the road to follow Terminus Place to a crossroads junction with River Road, crossing over into Mariners Quay, and go forward along an alleyway to reach a waterfront walk, looking upstream to the 1981 swing bridge

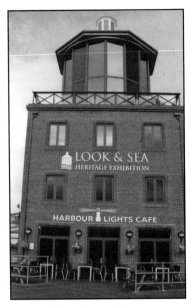

One of Littlehampton's more recent waterfront attractions

over the Arun. Here turn left to walk past smart new housing developments along the east bank of the river; it seems a long time since the riverside was buzzing with commercial activity, huge tonnages of goods being imported and exported from the quaysides. Shortly you reach the Look and Sea heritage exhibition which is to your left, and having enjoyed the exhibition you should detour hard left here to reach shortly the junction of River Road and Surrey Street, a charming area with attractive red-brick houses, little park and unusual circular metal sculpture. Then continue along the waterfront, noting some unusual posts carrying seafood recipes, going forward to a pavement beside Pier Road. From there keep walking along a riverside promenade, passing Oyster Pond, now a leisure amenity but previously a storage basin for the oyster catch hauled in by local fishermen. Keep on past the Harbour Park amusement complex and walk on to East Pier; the bottom end of it is shaped like the bow of a ship and you can pretend you're on the Titanic! Having enjoyed lovely views towards the dunes across the river, walk back to join the seaside promenade and turn right to follow it, noting the mock windmill towering above the Windmill Entertainment Centre to the left, and a bit further along to the left, the extensive Green. Soon on your left on the promenade itself is the remarkable Long Bench with the "roller coaster" effects beneath a pair of shelters, the inspiration of local schoolchildren, the wooden slats bearing commemorations to loved ones. Carry on past the very distinctive East Beach café, described as having a sculptural quality, then beyond the Norfolk Gardens to the left, you reach Mewsbrook Park with its lovely lake and, to the left, a nature conservation area with a wide range of plant life and bird life. Return to the entrance and bear briefly left to get an excellent view, to the left, of the red-brick Rustington Convalescent Home with impressive clock tower, dating back to 1897. Now retrace your steps along the seafront beside Sea Road, but this time, as Sea Road swings sharply right, swing right with it past Norfolk Gardens. As it bends sharply left note Norfolk Road going straight on; a sign on a shop on the left up this road commemorates the fact Ronnie Barker got the inspiration for the sitcom *Open All Hours* from a shop here. However, your way is westwards beside The Green along the elegant South Terrace (where Barker lived), some of which dates back to the very start of the 19th century. You pass a junction with St Augustine Road – the author Ian Fleming was in charge of a wartime secret intelligence unit in a house on the corner here – and then turn right into Granville Road, the street name possibly inspiring the name of one of the *Open All Hours* characters! Turn right into Fitzalan Road then, at the roundabout by the library, left into Maltravers Drive; just before the next roundabout, bear right along Church Approach into the churchyard. Where the path forks, go left past (and possibly into) the modern church, built in Gothic style in the 1930s, to enter Church Street, then bear left to arrive at the town museum which contains brooches and pottery from local Roman villas. Go straight on into the High Street, following it on into Terminus Road, and shortly you'll reach the station which is on the right.

Littlehaven *(Line A, 3 miles, linear walk to Horsham: easy)*

From the station follow Rusper Road northwards but almost immediately turn left into Lower Barn Copse, simply choosing the path through the woods nearest to and parallel with the road. Emerge back onto the road and follow it until, roughly level with Gateford Drive going off to the right, you reach another area of woodland to your left. Follow alongside this until you reach a gate and a blue disc signed "Horsham Riverside Walk" and here turn left onto a path which very shortly joins up with the swiftly flowing Channells Brook coming in from the right. This is a particularly lovely spot, in the shade of woodland, and in spring the green of the surrounding vegetation is given variety by the white of wild garlic. Now follow an excellent riverside path, arriving at North Heath Bridge and turning left onto North Heath Lane to cross the river then immediately bear right onto a path which promptly crosses the river again, and your riverside walk resumes. Shortly you reach a meadow separating your path from the river; you could walk across the meadow along the right bank, but soon the path returns to the riverside and you follow it to Pondtail Road. Turn left along this road past the Rising Sun, a very attractive pub, and on under the railway, continuing to a T-junction with Warnham Road. Bear right to follow it past the Dog & Bacon pub (the name is thought to be a corruption of "Dorking Beacon!") and cross Warnham Mill Bridge, noting the lovely waterfall to your right. Just beyond is the entrance to the Warnham Local Nature Reserve, a 92-acre site with a 17-acre millpond dating back to the 15th century on which the poet Shelley is reputed to have learn to sail; the water wheel is still operable although a flour mill which was built in the 17th century closed in the 1930s. The site attracts

The waterfall at Warnham Mill Nature Reserve

a wealth of wildlife including tufted ducks, kingfishers, cormorants, herons, terns, owls, sparrowhawks and roe deer while plants include sneezewort, common knapweed, devil's bit scabious and water mint. Note that the reserve has a small admission charge. Walk back over the bridge but turn immediately right along the delightful path (signed Horsham Riverside Walks) on the left bank of Boldings Brook, and in about a quarter of a mile you reach a T-junction with a metalled path, leading to a footbridge to the right. However you turn left along the metalled path and now head half-left across the fairway of a golf course, just in front of the tee. Reaching the far side of the fairway you arrive at a sign pointing left showing a cycle route to Horsham; turn left to follow this route, crossing Redford Avenue into Spencers Place, going straight on into Kempshott Road. At the end turn right and then immediately left into West Parade, bear right onto Warnham Road, and very shortly at the traffic lights turn left up Hurst Road. Follow this for half a mile or so to its end at a roundabout, where you will arrive at Horsham station.

London Road *(Line C, 10 miles, linear walk to Brighton: strenuous)*

Take the Lewes-bound platform exit, going forward past a pub and turning right into Springfield Road. Follow it uphill to Ditchling Road, turning right and almost immediately left down the narrow and pavement-less Hollingdean Lane, turning sharp right and going forward down Hollingdean Road. You pass under the railway, cross straight over Lewes Road using the pedestrian crossing – following signs for the crematoria! – into Bear Road, and follow this very straight road uphill for nearly a mile until the road finally levels out. You pass a crematorium and cemetery, also go past Tenantry Down Road coming in from the right, and then turn hard right into Warren Road. At the first opportunity, turn left to reach the boundary fence with the racecourse then left again along a narrow and not terribly clear path, keeping the racecourse fence to your right. Cross Wilson Avenue and continue as before, a clear track now emerging as you walk; arrive at and walk through a car park to its very eastern end where you join a clear track, initially keeping the race course to your right then striking out south-eastwards, with East Brighton Golf Course to your right and a fence to your left. This is lovely open walking.

A little under half a mile from the car park turn left to pass through a gate and follow a path downhill to the valley bottom. You turn right along a signed path along the valley floor, then in a couple of hundred yards turn left onto a path which rises steeply, dropping to a T-junction with a track (1), turning right. However at (1) you may wish to detour hard right through a gate signed Access Land and climb back through the rough grass up to the hilltop to reach the Mount Pleasant trig point, enjoying lovely views to the surrounding coastline and downs. Then return to the track at (1) and turn right as stated above, following it to a T-junction, here turning right to follow Ovingdean Road downhill. As it bends left go straight on along a narrow road, following it round to the left to reach the lovely centre of the old village of Ovingdean with its beautiful flint cottages and clearly signed 11th century church with a stunning chancel arch. Follow the road on, kinking left then right, shortly bearing left into Ainsworth Avenue and following it uphill to a T-junction, turning right to follow Longhill Road briefly, then as it veers sharply right go straight on, immediately reaching a 3-way footpath fork. Take the middle path, a delightful ridge-top walk with great views to the sea and Rottingdean. Shortly detour to view the 18th century Rottingdean smock windmill; still boasting four sails, it was once used to store contraband goods as well as being a useful landmark to fishermen at sea.

Return to the path and go forward to join Sheep Walk, then turn left at the first crossroads, junction with Nevill Road. This shortly becomes a path then drops very steeply to reach Rottingdean High Street. Turn left and walk up the street past several rather attractive Georgian houses, the village green to your right; among the lovely houses by the green are North End House, sometime home of the

North End House, one of Rottingdean's finest houses

artist Edward Burne-Jones, and over the road across the green is the Elms where Rudyard Kipling, Burne-Jones' nephew, lived between 1897 and 1902. There's a well-signed "Kipling Garden" immediately adjacent. At the road junction at the top of the green veer round to the right, keeping the green with attractive pond to your right. To your left is the flint church of St Margaret, which is of Saxon foundation, and then the imposing Grange, the former vicarage and now a museum with several Kipling-related exhibits. Turn left onto the High Street and follow it past attractive houses and shops; on the right is the early 16th century Black Horse, the earliest complete secular building in the village and a popular meeting place for smugglers.

On reaching the coast road, cross using the pedestrian crossing and turn right, then just beyond the bus shelter bear left across the grass to join and follow an obvious green coast path heading uphill alongside the fence by the cliff edge. Then simply follow it along the clifftop, with superb views towards Brighton Marina, Brighton and beyond. Just before you get level with the Brighton Marina complex you'll see the buildings of Roedean, probably England's best known girls' private school, to your right. You pass well above Brighton Marina and enjoy excellent views to this 1970s complex of harbour, boats, shops and flats. You arrive at the end of the cliff path just by the western pedestrian entrance to the complex. Here you could detour to the complex by a zigzag route bringing you down to the marina level, returning to the higher level by a concrete walkway and then a climb, observing the cycle path signs for Kemp Town and Whitehawk and crossing the coast road by means of a pedestrian crossing; if you prefer not to detour, simply go forward to the pedestrian crossing! Having crossed, turn left along the far side of the coast road very briefly, then turn right into Lewes Crescent, soon passing the old Roedean School, founded as Wimbledon House. Pass the private gardens, known as the Kemp Town Enclosures, and soon arrive at a crossroads on what is Sussex Square. Turn left, then almost immediately left again round the west side of Lewes Crescent, then bear right along Chichester Terrace, then Clarendon Terrace, then Percival Terrace; this is the heart of Kemp Town, the opulent area of east Brighton created in the early 19th century by Thomas Kemp. You'll see one or two "blue plaques" for famous people who resided in houses here, including Richard Addinsell, composer of the Warsaw Concerto.

You return to the coast road briefly then within sight of the Bristol Arms pub sign, bear right into Eastern Terrace and right again into the attractive Paston Place; at the end you turn left into St George's Road but look straight ahead here to view the impressive front of the Royal Sussex Hospital. Now simply follow St George's Road with a plethora of independent shops, flea market and cafes along the streets, and lovely streets of Regency houses going off to the left, with great sea views. The road becomes Bristol Road then Upper St James's Street then St James's Street, at its end arriving at a T-junction with the Old Steyne. Go straight on over, past lovely gardens to the right and left, and continue up North Street; at the clock tower at the top, turn right into Queen's Road and follow it back to the station.

Moulsecoomb *(Line C, 2.5 miles, circular walk: moderate - NB. NO REFRESHMENTS)*

Take the Lewes-bound platform exit, using a concrete path, almost immediately turning left steeply up Crespin Way, shortly bearing hard right along Barrow Hill, then left at the top into Uplands Road. Shortly before the end, just beyond a school, bear right along a signed footpath/alleyway, soon arriving at Lynchet Close; go straight over onto a clear track heading for open countryside, with excellent views to central Brighton. The track narrows and becomes a path, veering half-right with a golf course to the left and following the left-hand edge of a broad expanse of open field. Follow the path all the way round to the top left corner of the open ground but just before the corner, bear left along a clear path (unsigned at this junction). Keep along the obvious path which veers gently right, keeping a fairway of the golf course to your left; you pass the green with yellow flag at the end of the fairway, then very shortly reach a crossroads of paths (1). Turn left along a path which passes the back of the green and goes up to a T-junction with another path, where a footpath finger post is situated. Bear left here, and then very soon turn right to arrive at the Hollingbury Castle circular embankment. The castle is a hill-fort which appears to have been constructed in the middle of the third century BC and abandoned in the middle of the second century BC. Now follow the embankment round, clockwise or anti-clockwise as

The view towards Brighton from Hollingbury Castle

you wish, but the views are magnificent, encompassing Brighton and the South Downs; it's a true panorama with a huge variety of landscapes.

When you've completed the circuit, retrace your steps to (1) below, but this time go straight over and almost at once reach a T-junction with another path, with an excellent view ahead. Turn right here and follow the path through woodlands, emerging to pass an attractive pond and go forward to a path junction with a fingerpost; bear left here to follow a clear green path downhill, keeping the open fields to the right. You need to aim for the bottom end of the open area where the two swathes of woodland meet (2), doing so either by sticking to the green field edge path or, in due course, joining a more direct but unsigned path straight for point (2). Having reached that point, go forward onto a clear path through the vegetation, arriving at a T-junction with a metalled path; turn right here, descend the steps and then rise gently to arrive back at the station.

Newhaven Harbour *(Line D, 3 miles, linear walk to Seaford: easy)*

Leave the station by turning right onto the adjacent Beach Road; as it bends sharply to the left by the railway, turn right onto a footpath, staying parallel with (to the land side of) the railway briefly then crossing the railway footbridge. Keep walking initially beside the railway, but very shortly turn right over a bridge across Mill Creek then bear left onto the signed path which follows the creek briefly, veering sharply right and, keeping buildings to the right, going forward to reach a shingle bank with the beach beyond. Bear right along the shingle to the mouth of the Ouse. From here you get excellent views back to Castle Hill and the cliffs below it, and it's worth walking to the end of the pier on the east side of the harbour mouth; it's a great place to watch boats coming in and out of the harbour, but take care as there are gaps in the fencing giving sheer drops from the pier to the sea.

Retrace your steps and head south-eastwards towards Seaford, choosing between the beach and a metalled track running behind it. If the tide's out, the beach is better as you can walk to the water's edge where the going is much firmer. The track however soon passes the site of the abandoned village of Tide Mills, and it's certainly worth detouring up the signed path to view the ruins more closely; in its heyday it consisted of a large tide mill and cottages housing about a hundred workers. The mill stopped in around 1900 and the village was condemned as unfit for habitation in 1936, the last residents leaving in 1939.

Beyond the sailing club building, which is very distinctive and easy to make out whichever route you take, join the Bonningstedt Promenade past the sprawling Bishopstone which is to the left, and go forward to the buildings of Seaford, keeping Marine Parade then the Esplanade to the left. As you get level with the impressive old redbrick Stratheden Court, which dominates the seafront, leave the promenade and cross over the Esplanade to follow West View (immediately west of Stratheden). Veer very slightly left up Pelham

Looking towards the ruins of Tide Mills

Road, noting the attractive white-painted Smugglers Cottage and Wey Cottage to your right, then turn right at the end at Dane Road and follow it to a junction with the A259, meeting here the top of Church Street. Turn hard right into Church Street and left into Place Lane, which brings you to Broad Street, the town's principal shopping area. Turn right to walk down it, passing the Croft Lane turning to the left – it's worth detouring into it to view the impressive brick almshouses – then bear right into the High Street. Pass the red-brick Regency Restaurant, over 200 years old, on the left, and a little further down on the right, the still older Old House, sometime home of the Seaford bailiff. Now retrace your steps a little and almost opposite the Regency Restaurant turn left up a narrow alley and on through the grounds of St Leonard's Church, perhaps detouring to visit it with its Norman features including nave and clerestory window. Then bear westwards, turning right into Church Street, following it uphill to reach the A259 and turning left here to reach the station.

Newhaven Town *(Line D, 3 miles, circular walk: easy)*

Exit the station and turn immediately left onto Drove Road, going forward onto the A259 to cross the swing bridge over the Ouse. Immediately beyond the bridge, turn left onto Riverside and proceed beside the Ouse along the right bank downstream. There is great variety including areas of green, ingeniously carved signposts, modern developments, the Ark pub with its beautifully painted sign on the wall, and, on the water, fishing vessels and perhaps a Transmanche ferry in port. At one time a significant commodity unloaded here was ice imported from the Baltic and supplied to local businesses. You veer right on the approach to

Newhaven Marina, turning left to follow Fort Road for a couple of hundred yards, soon reaching the Newhaven Fort entrances and turning right up the pedestrian one. (Note that if you decide not to visit the fort, or it's shut, the walk continues at * by your turning right into the car park.) Completed during the 1860s as a response to the threat of French invasion, the fort is of interest in its own right with its ramparts, underground tunnels, sturdy brick buildings, ammunition stores and gun emplacements, and from beside the guns at the highest point there are fantastic views. However it also houses excellent exhibitions and memorabilia devoted to the two world wars, especially World War II, with particularly good sections on the home front, the Normandy landings and also the disastrous Dieppe raid of 1942 which was launched from Newhaven. You can relive the terrifying approach of a V1 flying bomb (doodlebug), the sneering of Lord Haw-Haw, and the singing of Flanagan & Allen, and there's also an excellent café and shop. After your visit, emerge from the exit and turn hard left into the car park.

*Follow the walkway up and past the left-hand side of the car park, then veer away from the walkway up a bank to reach a circular area of seating. Turn left onto a metalled pathway which climbs steadily, then as it veers to the right, bear left onto a path which proceeds through the trees to emerge on the top of Castle Hill. You now veer right to enjoy a really lovely walk along the cliffs, with breathtaking views to Newhaven town, harbour, Seaford Head and the South Downs; its enjoyment value is in the sheer variety of urban and rural landscapes and landmarks. You pass the coastguard lookout and the mast which towers above it, continuing to an area of seating, here looking out for and turning hard right onto a pathway which keeps the mast your right. Note the narrow alleys linking this pathway with the clifftop, part of the elaborate defensive fortifications that extend beyond the Fort itself.

One of the many features of interest at Newhaven Fort

Just beyond the mast, look out for and turn left onto a path which drops steeply downhill in woodland through what is now part of a nature reserve. Observing all the signs, descend to a large parking area; turn right to follow

the car park to a T-junction with the Fort approach road for vehicles, bearing left here and following it downhill to Fort Road.

Now turn right to follow Fort Road past Hope Inn as far as a parking area at the western entrance to the harbour. The breakwater leading to the lighthouse may be closed to the public but you can enjoy a bracing stroll on the shingle instead, and from the waterfront by the parking area there are excellent views across the harbour mouth and eastwards to the cliffs of Seaford Head. Now return to Fort Road and retrace your steps, turning right into West Quay and then following the waterfront to the swing bridge; having re-crossed the bridge, veer right down Drove Road to return to the station.

There's another excellent museum/themed exhibition a short walk from Newhaven Town station. To reach it, carry on past the station and over the crossing, then cross to the north side of the main road and continue briefly on beyond the railway, turning left onto New Road (A26) and continuing alongside an industrial estate. Shortly before the road bends to the right, turn right off the A26 onto another New Road then bear right again to follow Avis Road briefly to Paradise Park which is to your right. Here you'll find the Museum of Life, tracing the history of life from millions of years ago with life-size dinosaurs and exhibitions devoted to sea life and Neanderthal times. There is a huge collection of the world's flora and there's also a history trail and beautiful gardens with many fine water features. Continue a short distance, turn right into Avis Way and almost immediately right again onto a path, returning to the A26 then retracing your steps back to the station.

Normans Bay *(Line C, 10 miles, circular walk: strenuous)*

Note: The paths here are very faint and helpful landmarks are scarce so a clear day is a must. As you'll be retracing your steps from point (1) below, note what landmarks there are to ensure you retrace accurately.

Turn left from the station exit and follow the road away from the sea, almost immediately turning right at a T-junction, crossing over an artificial channel known as Waller's Haven and soon reaching the Star Inn which is to the left. The inn, once a smugglers' haunt, is thought to date from the 15th century when Waller's Haven was cut. Beyond the pub you pass the signed driveway to the pub car park and immediately beyond that you join a signed footpath going off to the left, fractionally west of north, entering the area of grass and marshland known as the Pevensey Levels. Walk through a field to a stile, and forward from there along the right side of another field to a further stile, beyond which, veering just east of north, you follow a reasonably well defined path between two narrow channels of water. You

The beautiful country church at Hooe

arrive at a footbridge and profusion of gates, and here veer just west of north again aiming for a footbridge with a yellow post; the line is the mast you can see on the hillside behind. There's no path, so just follow the rough grass, enjoying pleasant walking, with very good views towards Eastbourne and Beachy Head. You cross the footbridge and continue in the same direction, aiming for another yellow post, again the line being the mast. You arrive at a dirt track, turning right and crossing a channel then reaching a footpath crossroads (1) and going straight over, crossing a stile. Now you need to aim half-right, pretty much due north, and should identify the next footbridge with no difficulty, heading for and crossing that (again no path). From there you make for a gate (adjacent to another footbridge), again heading north, your line being the far left-hand end of the big farm complex on the hillside. Once again there's no path. Go forward to and through the gate and over this (fifth!) footbridge, entering a field and veering just west of north to its far end, aiming for a gate. Cross the stile by the gate then turn left onto a narrow lane; turn left onto the lane then shortly bear right onto a lane which brings you to the A259.

Cross straight over the A259 with care, to follow a road signed Hooe, uphill past New Lodge Farm, then take the first road turning to the left about a quarter of a mile beyond the farm. Just beyond the splendid Court Lodge with its magnificent topiary, turn right onto a footpath which follows the right-hand field edge downhill, then rises. The path is far from clear on the ground as you ascend, but stick to the right-hand field edge. At the top, turn left to follow the field edge round along the ridge, entering another field and then shortly bearing right, as signed, to reach Hooe church. It has one of the most idyllic settings of any country church, its chief treasure being a supposedly Saxon muniment chest.

Follow the churchyard round to the left of the main entrance as you face it, up to the top left corner, going through a gate to join a signed path, turning left. Follow the left-hand field edge, going forward into another field and maintaining the left-hand edge; woodland now takes over to your left, and your path then enters the wood and becomes a clear track arriving at a T-junction with a narrow road. Turn right onto it, immediately turning left onto the B2095 Pevensey-Battle road then very shortly bear right onto Horsewalk, a narrow and very pretty metalled road, soon commanding excellent views. You descend to a valley bottom and walk along the road as far as a redbrick bridge over Waller's Haven; immediately beyond the bridge crossing, bear left to join a signed footpath which heads westwards through fields. You cross a couple of fields as signed, bear shortly right onto a track then immediately left along a left-hand field edge, following it round to the right, keeping a patch of woodland ahead of you and to your half-right. Look out for and take a signed path going left, rising to reach a clearer path then veering right along this path, contouring the hillside and taking an obvious course through fields to reach Wartling. Turn right onto a lane, going forward to a junction with a road by the pretty Lamb Inn. Your way is northwards downhill along the road signed for Herstmonceux but it's worth detouring left to inspect the very pretty church with its box pews, and superb views towards Eastbourne from the churchyard.

Now follow the Herstmonceux road for just over a quarter of a mile until you reach Coopers Farm which is to your left. Don't take the first track but turn left as signed onto a footpath which initially keeps a fence to the left then goes downhill, with thick vegetation on each side. You pull clear of this and follow the right-hand edge of the fields, but look out for and take (before reaching the valley bottom) a signed path heading right. Follow it clearly across a field then along the left-hand edge of a wood, emerging and turning right at a path fork, following an often faint squelchy path along the right-hand edge of the meadows with trees to the right. In half a mile or so, as you approach an apparent dead end, make for and cross a gate and stile to your left. Don't go straight ahead on the farm track, rather fork right immediately beyond the gate along a path which rises gently through pasture. You're soon reassured by a signpost, reaching a signed junction with the 1066 Country Walk. Your way is right, eastwards, along the 1066 route but you should continue a little further to get the best view of Herstmonceux Castle and its moat, although access to the castle itself is forbidden from here. Originally built in 1440, Herstmonceux was one of the first and largest brick buildings in England, and despite restoration, the original battlements and turrets remain to this day.

Follow the 1066 route eastwards on a clear path, climbing and walking through woodland, reaching a road; immediately to the left here is the entrance to the Science Centre and castle should you wish to visit them. With its domes and telescopes, the Science Centre is part of the former home of the Royal Greenwich

Observatory and is one of the country's leading Science Centres with more than 100 exciting interactive exhibits. However your station walk bears right along the road which takes you back to Wartling. At the Lamb Inn don't bend right but go straight on, turning shortly left to follow Horsewalk, a lovely quiet road through beautiful countryside with excellent views towards Hooe. On returning to the brick bridge over Waller's Haven, cross it and turn immediately right through the long grass, then veer left as signed. Walk briefly eastwards, parallel with the road, crossing into another field and bearing right here, just east of south, across the meadow on a very faint path. Following a line of telegraph poles you go over a stile into the next field where the path becomes clearer, and you continue south-eastwards across the field to arrive at a road. Turn left onto it and then almost immediately right onto the B2095 past another Lamb Inn, to reach the A259.

Cross it then turn right to briefly follow beside it, but in a few yards, just before the bridge over Waterlot Stream, turn left to join a path parallel with the stream. Initially unpromising, it soon becomes a good clear grassy embankment path. In a few hundred yards you reach a gate, going through it and reaching a T-junction with a track, turning right to continue beside the stream. Very soon however the stream veers to the right again, at another gate; don't go through the gate but turn left as signed through rough grass, and go over a stile. Now once more you need to concentrate! Look to the horizon for the furthermost tree on the same vertical line as the stile is pointing, and just to the right of that line, you should see a telegraph pole on the horizon and a little nearer to you (on the line of the telegraph pole) a post. Make your way across the pasture to reach the post – there is a faint path in places but don't rely on it – then continue through the meadow south-eastwards in the direction indicated by the arrow sign on the post, keeping some trees just to your right, and looking out carefully for a gate in the fence to the right in a couple of hundred yards. Here, go through into the next field and again following the south-easterly direction shown by the arrow, continue through the pasture. To your right is a rise, the site of the now non-existent medieval village of Northeye, and shortly you reach the footpath crossroads indicated at (1) above. Turn right here then, having immediately crossed the footbridge using the dirt track, you reach the yellow post and now retrace your steps to Normans Bay.

Nutbourne *(Line A, 13 miles, linear walk to Chichester: strenuous)*

Turn left from either platform exit along Broad Road and walk northwards into the village of Hambrook, veering north-eastwards to cross the A27; turn left immediately beyond it along a path which runs parallel with it and shortly reaches the south end of metalled Hambrook Hill North. Turn right to follow this road, going straight over West Ashling Road onto a footpath which heads pleasantly northwards through woodland, arriving at Common Road. Cross with care and turn left beside the boundary fence of a research establishment, then immediately beyond the far end of the establishment grounds, bear right onto a signed footpath. This initially hugs the boundary fence, heading north but veering north-eastwards, then strikes out just east of north through trees, gradually gaining height and arriving at Hares Lane.

Turn right to follow this lane for just under half a mile, then bear left onto a lane signed Adsdean to the left, soon turning right at a fork junction onto a signed bridleway. Very shortly you reach another fork junction by a gravel pit, this time turning left and shortly veering north-eastwards. You swing briefly just south of east, passing a path coming in from the left, then veer resolutely north-eastwards and now climb onto Funtington Down on an excellent path; it's a pretty relentless ascent but the surrounding woodland is extremely attractive. For a while you're skirting the right-hand edge of woods but then enter the thicker part of Hounsom Firs, eventually reaching a path T-junction after a mile of almost solid climbing.

Bear right at this junction and follow the path, emerging from the woods and following its left fringe, arriving at a path junction (1). Signage suggests you should carry straight on, plunging back into the woods and losing height, then in a couple of hundred yards turning hard left up a signed bridlepath bringing you to another junction (2). However there seems nothing to stop you following the much more direct stony field-edge path round to the left at (1) to reach (2) very shortly! Then continue north-westwards from (2) on the stony path along the edge of the trees to shortly reach a junction with a path going off to the right into the woods. At this junction you're 181m (nearly 600ft) above sea level compared with 9m (roughly 30ft) at the start.

Turn right along the path, now in Kingley Vale Nature Reserve, particularly well known for its yew woods, and one of the most unspoilt and beautiful pieces of countryside in West Sussex, observable from miles away because of its great height in comparison with the low-lying harbour area to the south. The path heads north-eastwards through the woods, emerging at an open area close to burial mounds known as the Devil's Humps from which your earlier endeavours are rewarded with fabulous views down to Chichester and Chichester Harbour. Continue on into further woodland, veering eastwards then northwards to pass the Bow Hill trig point and shortly arriving at a crossroads of paths. Turn right here and join a path which begins to descend, emerging from the wood to give more tremendous views south towards Chichester and the surrounding countryside. Continue to lose height and head just east of south through open country to reach a crossroads of paths, bearing left here and heading eastwards then just east of north to arrive at a crossing of the B2141 Lavant-South Harting road. Turn right then almost immediately left onto Binderton Lane, climbing at first then descending to the A286.

Cross with care, bearing right and, just by the bus stop, shortly left down a path heading gently downhill to the floor of the Lavant valley – you may be lucky enough to see the lovely river Lavant flowing just here – and having crossed the course of the river you reach a path fork. Don't fork right with the Centurion Way but continue straight on, crossing the old Chichester-Midhurst railway and going forward to a signed path junction. Go over the crossing path onto a fainter but still clear path which heads steeply up the grassy hillside, heading north-eastwards. Now veering right you follow a clear path up a gentler gradient, enjoying magnificent views towards Chichester and the coast. You pass a splendidly placed hilltop house and very shortly beyond it reach another signed multi-path junction, with Chalkpit Lane falling away steeply to the right here. Go straight over onto the stony track signed Trundle, heading uphill; you pass through a gate, and at the junction of paths a little beyond, take the one heading onto the perimeter path circling this magnificent Iron Age hillfort. Follow the perimeter path round then turn left to follow a path which takes you to the triangulation point in the fort centre – even better views are available from a hillock immediately adjacent – then continue along this narrow path to reach the perimeter path at the other end, and turn right to follow the perimeter path back round to where you initially joined it. The views are absolutely stupendous on a clear day; the Isle of Wight and Spinnaker Tower are clearly visible to the west, and there's then a huge swathe of coastline on show, which may extend as far as the Seven Sisters! Now retrace your steps down to the multi-path junction, and turn left to follow the sign for Lavant down Chalkpit Lane, heading southwards. At the T-junction with a road turn right to follow it through the very pretty village of East Lavant past the Royal Oak and the medieval church of St Mary with sturdy brick tower; cross a bridge over the river Lavant and then turn immediately right up Sheepwash Lane, keeping the river Lavant to your right and the village green to your left, and climb to reach the A286. Turn right to walk beside it briefly, soon reaching what looks like a church lychgate. Pass through it and walk down the slope, passing the former Lavant railway station which is to your right; just beyond the old station, turn right into Warbleheath Close and arrive on the course of the old Chichester-Midhurst Railway, now the Centurion Way footpath/cycleway. The old railway opened in 1881 and closed to passengers in 1935, but continued to be used for freight, and one section was open as comparatively recently as between 1972 and 1991 for coal transport. Turn right to follow it, and simply keep on along it for two and a half miles or so. Once you've left the buildings of Lavant behind, the surroundings become delightfully rural, and continue to be very pleasant as you continue just west of the northern fringes of Chichester past Brandy Hole Copse, to just short of the point where the course of the old railway meets the still extant Chichester-Havant railway. Here you veer left past the buildings of

A lovely stretch of the Centurion Way just south of Lavant

Bishop Luffa School, turning left onto a metalled road to reach the junction of Sherborne Road, Westgate and Cathedral Way. Bear half-right to follow the footpath/cycle path beside Via Ravenna, keeping Chichester College to the left, then immediately beyond the next roundabout by the Westgate Leisure Centre, cross over to follow a path along the right-hand side of the Avenue de Chartres. Shortly the path forks: take the right fork alongside the Waitrose car park, and reach a T-junction of paths, turning right, keeping Waitrose immediately to your right, and the multi-storey car park to your left. Follow the path with the multi-storey still to your left, and veer right to arrive at Chichester station.

Ore *(Line C, 7.5 miles, linear walk to Hastings: strenuous)*

Proceed from the station up the long slipway, turning left at the end along Hughenden Road and left at the T-junction along Mount Pleasant Road. Go straight on into Priory Road and follow it to its end as it meets the A259 Old London Road. Turn left to follow this road for a little under half a mile, arriving in the centre of Ore, and opposite Christ Church bear right to follow Fairlight Road just north of east then in just over half a mile bear left into Beacon Road, heading north-eastwards. The road becomes a path and climbs quite steeply, arriving at a junction with a track (1). The continuous route bears right here along the track, but you should turn left to immediately arrive at an area of green with topograph, this being North's Seat. At nearly 600ft it's the highest point in the Hastings area and a magnificent viewpoint with a panorama which will include not only Hastings itself but a large area of the surrounding coastline and the Weald; it's claimed that the north coast of France can be seen with the naked eye on a clear day. Return to the track you met at (1) and go straight on along it, almost immediately crossing a road to join a footpath through the trees. At the fork junction take the right fork, emerging from the trees and crossing a field; go straight over Fairlight Road onto a metalled path which drops downhill and in a few hundred yards reaches a path junction with no right of way ahead. Turn left here onto the footpath. You go straight over another path junction, and you can see a mast straight ahead; shortly beyond this junction your path veers noticeably to the right, and climbs to reach a gate giving access to an area of green at the end of which is the mast. There's a path signpost here with the number 23 and a taller post advertising "Firehills 150m, Car Parks 300m." Here you turn sharply right, seawards, along a path which follows the edge of the green, keeping a fence to the right, and arrives level with but below the mast. You reach a junction of paths here, where you turn right to join what is the coast path heading back towards Hastings. The views as you begin are breathtaking.

There are a lot of paths leading off the main one but the golden rule is to stick to the one closest to the sea and, where there are signposts, follow the path as signed for Hastings. In practice you won't go wrong, and you can enjoy two and a half fantastic miles in which you negotiate three glens (valleys), enjoying wonderful cliff and woodland views and a huge variety of vegetation and bird life. You begin with a descent to Warren Glen, less thickly wooded than the other two glens you have to follow but still populated with oak, hazel, beech and ash. Then there's a stiff climb – there is a path pointing seawards as you ascend, and you do ignore that one – and a brief level section, then down you go again, into Fairlight Glen, bearing

Spectacular cliff scenery between Firehills and Hastings

left as signed. You're some way back from the sea here, erosion having taken its toll on earlier cliff paths, but the views remain magnificent as you drop down to the valley stream in the shade of trees and surrounded by large boulders. This is arguably the loveliest of the three glens, with beautiful woodland carpeted in spring with bluebells and wood anemones. You ascend again to follow a level grassy path, but then there's a really steep descent – thankfully steps are provided – to Ecclesbourne Glen, a wooded valley that 200 years ago was popular with smugglers and which provides ideal nesting territory for tits and warblers. The valley bottom is almost absurdly narrow, and almost at once you begin climbing again, to reach the top of East Hill. Follow the cliff path to its far end, passing the funicular railway entrance and going back down the steps to Tackleway; go straight over down Crown Lane and left into All Saints Street, arriving at the junction of Rock-a-Nore Road with the main coast road (A259). Turn right to walk beside the coast road on the inland side until you reach the roundabout junction at Breeds Place. Fork half-right here to enter the main shopping complex, passing under Albert Road and entering Wellington Place. To reach the station, bear right as signed into Havelock Road.

Pevensey & Westham *(Line C, 4 miles, circular walk: easy)*

(This also covers Pevensey Bay - it is recommended that you continue straight on to Pevensey Bay station; the walk is described on that basis and 4 miles is the aggregate for both)

Leave the station by turning right onto the B2191 Eastbourne Road, then very shortly right onto High Street (pub and shop available), now in the village of Westham. You pass two really fine timber-framed houses, including the Old Dial House, and the splendid church of St Mary, believed to be the first church the Normans built in England and boasting a particularly impressive 14th century tower. As the main street veers left, continue straight on to follow a path through the precincts of Pevensey Castle, built by the Normans but previously the site of the great Roman fortress of Anderida; it continued to be garrisoned until the 14th century and was re-fortified during the Spanish Armada and again during World War II. The "inner ward" which carries an admission charge, is easily seen and accessed to the right of the path.

At the far end, go on into Pevensey High Street. In the Platagenet era, Pevensey was actually a seaport most notably for exporting Wealden iron and actually became one of the Cinque Ports but was subsequently a victim of silting. You very shortly pass the tile-hung 14th century Mint House which is to your left, and, a little further down, the former Town Hall, claimed to be the smallest in England, which is to your right. The building, now a museum, was also once a court house. Continue

The Court House at Pevensey

to the end of the High Street, turning right into Wallsend Road (A259). However very shortly turn right into Church Lane, past an area of modern housing; you kink right by the impressive Glebe House, and then left, proceeding pleasantly past the imposing Marsh Hall to the Early English church of St Nicolas, completely uniform 13th century, which is to the left. Opposite the church gate, bear right to arrive back at the High Street by the Town Hall. You could simply retrace your steps to Pevensey & Westham station from here, turning left to head back up to the castle arch, but the recommended walk goes straight on to Pevensey Bay station to pick up the undemanding and enjoyable Pevensey Bay station walk, as follows. Turn right rather than left by the Town Hall, walk down the High Street once again and turn right at the end into Wallsend Road (A259), this time continuing to Pevensey Bay station.

From this station, head seawards along Wallsend Road, but very shortly turn right onto a path, just beyond a garage. Go initially alongside the garage buildings, then veer left with the path, going forward to a footbridge and arriving at a field with an embankment along its right-hand nearside edge. The OS map shows the right of way as following diagonally across the field but there's no path so I suggest you go anti-clockwise round the edge of the field via the embankment, arriving at a metalled gate at the far right-hand corner. Go through the gate along a narrow stony path, continuing forward to cross a road and following the path (note the "no cycling" sign) to the Castle Inn by the main road through Pevensey Bay village, Eastbourne Road A259. You cross the road and the continuous route turns left(north-eastwards) here, but it's worth detouring briefly right then left into Leyland Road on which is a very well preserved Martello tower. You will see three of these distinctive round constructions on this walk; there were 74 built along the south coast, prompted by the renewed threat of French invasion in 1806.

Now follow Eastbourne Road north-eastwards, remaining on the seaward side, and just beyond a modern church bear right along Collier Road to the beach. Turn right here along the shingle, enjoying excellent views to Sovereign Harbour and

Beachy Head, with two more Martello towers in view. You have to veer left and round a stone wall where buildings protrude further seaward than those previously, and it's a little way past the wall that you get level with another Martello tower to your right, this time of sturdy red brick. Use a concrete walkway to walk down to it, bearing left onto the road beyond the tower. You then shortly bear right onto Timberlaine Road, bringing you back to the A259 which you cross with care, turning left and almost immediately right onto a path signed Pevensey Castle. You follow the left bank of a narrow channel, crossing a footbridge and now following a wider channel, the inelegantly named Langney Sewer. In a few hundred yards you cross a metalled footbridge and just beyond here your path veers left, becoming less distinct, aiming for St Mary's church, Westham. Cross the railway and follow the left-hand edge of a field beyond. A footpath sign reassures you as you continue on a clear path to the left of the churchyard of St Mary's and then the church itself. You arrive at Westham High Street, turning left to retrace your steps to Pevensey & Westham station.

A Martello Tower in a distinctly suburban setting

Plumpton *(Line F, 6 miles, linear walk to Lewes: strenuous)*

From the main station exit on the down platform, turn immediately right onto Station Road, going over the level crossing and following Station Road southwards for just over half a mile, keeping Plumpton racecourse to your right. You reach a crossroads of driveways; turn right signposted for the Plumpton health complex, alongside the south end of the racecourse with lovely views to the Downs to your left. Ignore a path going off to the right, then just before a group of buildings to the left, bear left onto a signed footpath. This proceeds clearly southwards, soon reaching two footbridges; cross both and go forward along a right-hand field edge, and where the field-edge path ends, kink slightly right to join a farm lane. This continues clearly southwards for half a mile or so, ignoring paths leading off, passing the buildings of the agricultural college. As the lane, now a driveway, veers left by the bus stop, you could detour right along a footpath for a few hundred yards to reach the old flint Norman church of St Michael. Whether you've detoured or not, follow the driveway uphill towards the road ahead. Shortly before the road junction there's another detour opportunity to the left, to see the beautiful lakes and buildings of 16th century Plumpton Place; neither house nor grounds open to the public, so admire them from the footpath. Then walk up the driveway to the busy B2116 and cross over, bearing right then immediately left up a signed bridleway. Follow it uphill, initially just west of south, then veering sharply eastwards; this is hard work and gets tougher. You reach a T-junction with a track, turning right onto it then bear shortly left onto a signed bridleway which now climbs very steeply and continues uphill south-eastwards. After a final push you make it to the South Downs Way (SDW), turning left to follow it, along the top of the escarpment. The views are astonishing, the buildings of Brighton visible on a clear day. You dip down slightly, parting company with the SDW which darts away to the right, and then rise again, keeping to the right of the trees but as close to the top of the escarpment as possible, reaching the trig point at the summit of Blackcap. Pause to enjoy more quite magnificent views, then continue straight ahead downhill from the trig point, very shortly reaching a crossroads of tracks, and here forking gently left to continue downhill. Having reached the bottom, ignoring paths leading away right and left, you begin climbing again, with trees and bushes dotting the hillside around you. As the path levels out and you emerge from the trees, fork right away from the bridleway and make for the beacon, erected to commemorate the Queen's Golden Jubilee in 2002.

The Jubilee Beacon on Mount Harry

This is the summit of Mount Harry, the best views being eastwards to the hills above Lewes, the Ouse valley and the South Downs escarpment east of the Ouse climaxing in Firle Beacon.

Follow the clear path eastwards beyond the beacon downhill, soon being reunited with the green track which is now signed as a bridleway. You continue to descend, passing under a line of pylons and proceeding south-eastwards round the top edge of a steep tree-lined hillside, the bridleway clear throughout. You arrive at a gate and enter a field, with the bridleway veering round to the left beside the trees, but you join another, unsigned, path which strikes out across the middle of the field, rising to reach a gate in the fence, passing through it and bearing right to pass through a second gate. Now turn right,

The glorious ascent onto the South Downs near Blackcap

keeping a dark wooden fence (and stables beyond) to your left, and soon reach a T-junction with a bridleway signed SDW to the right and Lewes to the left. Now follow the bridleway eastwards towards Lewes, passing the stables which are to the right. The surface becomes rougher and the path narrower, but once you've passed over a crossing track the going is clear, easy and downhill all the way! Still enjoying excellent views to Lewes and beyond, keep descending, veering eastwards and passing just to the left of Lewes Prison to reach the A275. Cross straight over into Spital Road, going forward into Western Road (A277), soon passing the lovely Norman church of St Anne which is to the right, and the splendid Shelleys and old Grammar School to the left. Continue into the High Street, following it to the crossroads junction in the very centre of the town with Station Street going off to the right. Follow it steeply downhill and continue on to the station.

Polegate *(Line C, 6 miles, linear walk to Berwick: moderate)*

From the main station exit, turn left and walk the short distance to Polegate High Street, turning right to follow it northwards to a T-junction with the B2247. Turn right here then very shortly left into School Lane. As this road bends left, go straight on along the Cuckoo Trail as signposted and now follow this trail briefly, descending and soon crossing the A27. Immediately after crossing it, turn left onto the signed cycle route 2 which proceeds beside the A27. Don't be tempted away to the right but continue along route 2 as signed, passing under the A22 close to its junction with the A27, and veering right, briefly parallel with the A22. However you soon veer left as signed along route 2, following it north-westwards through attractive woodland. You reach a crossroads with Robin Post Lane where route two turns left, south-westwards; however you continue north-westwards along an often very muddy path, ignoring crossing tracks. You pass an open area that's to your left and plough on through the woods to arrive at the hamlet of Caneheath, turning right along the road, passing the Old Oak Inn then at Primrose Farm turning left as signed onto a track heading north-westwards. The track peters out at a field boundary but you continue as signed along a path which continues north-westwards, downhill; you cross into another field and pass under pylon lines, entering a further field to arrive just short of Mill Wood. Don't go forward to the tempting stile ahead but go half-left through the field to a gate, and beyond it bear right to follow a clear path along the far (west) edge of the wood, soon passing a signed path junction (1); keep on along the wood edge, veering left just at the end to arrive at Arlington Road West. Turn left onto it, almost immediately reaching Michelham Priory. The priory dates back to 1229 when Augustinian canons arrived, taking over the site of a moated Norman manor house, and it was dissolved in 1536. Apart from a 14th century gatehouse the priory buildings are not obviously medieval, as the later stonework of a Tudor farmhouse masks what survives of the original priory. The Tudor rooms are furnished with an excellent collection of Dutch paintings, Flemish tapestries and Old English furniture. The garden was constructed on the moated site of the old priory, and is packed with colour and variety including exotic waterside plants and sweeping herbaceous borders.

  Retrace your steps to (1) but now strike out across the field, arriving at the bank of the Cuckmere River. Continue beside it briefly, following the path carefully along the right-hand edge of a field, then as the river veers away to the right, you bear slightly left with the path, passing through a very pretty patch of woodland and emerging into a field. Now the going becomes straightforward, your path, which is clearly defined, rising and staying along the left-hand edge of the field. You enter another field, enjoying superb views forward to the Downs, and strike out half-right as signed across the field under pylon lines to enter a plantation, then bear left to leave the plantation and pass through another field, going forward to a T-junction with Tye Hill Road. Turn right then almost immediately left along a clear path on a right-hand field edge then left-hand field edge, arriving at a fork junction. Take the right fork which heads downhill, aiming for Arlington Church; keep immediately to the left of the pylon as you pass underneath the lines, avoiding being tempted to the right. At the bottom of the hill, cross a footbridge then enter the churchyard, keeping the church to your right. The path heads for the churchyard entrance but you may well wish to detour to visit the

Saxon church with Anglo-Saxon nave, Norman north chapel, and remains of medieval wall paintings. You arrive at the road, turning right (you may also wish to detour to visit the Yew Tree pub which is to the left!). Now follow the signed Wealdway across a field of rough grass, then just beyond the next field boundary turn right onto a signed path following right-hand field edges and going forward to cross the Cuckmere River by an impressive footbridge. From here proceed north-westwards as signed on an excellent path to Arlington Reservoir. Turn left to follow the reservoir round; as well as providing water for nearby Eastbourne, it's a wonderful wildlife haven and there are tremendous views back to Arlington and forward to the Downs. At the bottom (south) corner bear left onto a lane, then having soon passed a left path turn, take a right path turn, heading uphill along a left-hand field edge. Continue as signed downhill; as you descend you can see the obvious westward course of the path along the ground as it proceeds through fields and passes between buildings to reach Station Road. Turn left, past the Berwick village stores, and shortly right to arrive at Berwick station.

Portslade *(Line B, 6 miles, circular walk: moderate)*

From the Brighton-bound platform, go down to Station Road and cross straight over into Victoria Road, following it past the elegant red brick Portslade Town Hall and shortly reaching the Victoria Recreation Ground to the right. Turn right to follow a path which skirts the right-hand fringe of the green, but immediately beyond the children's play area bear left and walk across the recreation ground to the far right-hand (north-west) corner. Go forward along a subway under the A270, turning left up the ramp and, at the top, bear right into Locks Hill, following it to the centre of Old Portslade. The road swings left, but by detouring right into Manor Road you immediately arrive at the entrance of the very pretty flint built church of St Nicolas which dates back to the 12th century and boasts a 13th century chancel and tower. However the continuous route swings left, as stated; note a number of attractive cottages on each side, especially the white Alma Cottage and the flint-built Robins Row to the left. Now in South Street, you veer right to reach a junction with High Street, noting the very pretty Stags Head pub just over the road to the left, while immediately ahead is an old stock-brick factory building and factory chimney with carving near the base and the date 1881. Turn right up the High Street, immediately passing a line of very sweet cottages, nos 44-50, of which Copy Cottage, no 48, is perhaps the prettiest, and also look up at the lettering on the fine white house behind, 1805 OLD VILLAGE STORES, FAMILY GROCER AND PROVISIONS. A little further up, the white houses at nos 57 and 61, and the

The sign says it all!

flint creeper-clad 65 and 67, are most attractive.

Follow High Street round to the left to reach a junction with Drove Road. The continuous route turns left, just south of west, onto Drove Road but it's worth detouring right to visit Emmaus, a project designed to help homeless people in Brighton; it includes a "second-hand superstore," beautiful gardens, chapel and café with profits going to the charity. Whether you've detoured or not, now follow Drove Road just south of west, past turnings to Southdown Road and North Road to reach Valley Road. Turn right and then immediately left into Drove Crescent, bearing left after hundred yards along a narrow alleyway which rises to meet Mile Oak Road. Here bear right along Mile Oak Road, heading just west of north, past a pub and shop, to the very end, going forward to pass under the A27 road bridge and continuing past the Mile Oak Farm buildings. Shortly beyond these you reach a junction of paths, bearing right onto a signed bridleway which now heads north-eastwards, ascending and passing a dewpond which is to the left. Continue uphill north-eastwards, keeping Cockroost Hill to your right, then veer just north of east, descending to another T-junction of paths. Turn right and follow the path south-eastwards, rising gently and arriving at a trig point at the hilltop in the adjacent field on the left, with magnificent views to Brighton and the sea. Keep on the path which veers left and drops to reach the A27 footbridge which you cross, then continue on the obvious path south-eastwards to pass the very conspicuous and distinctive 1909 Foredown Tower.

Remain on the path beyond Foredown Tower, arriving at a junction with Fox Way, and turn left to follow it downhill, going straight over a roundabout into Hangleton Lane and following it to the crossroads junction with Hangleton Valley Drive. Turn right and almost at once arrive at the flint-built Hangleton Manor which is on the left. Now a restaurant, it's the oldest surviving domestic secular building in Brighton & Hove, dating back to 1540 and boasting 16th century panelling and flooring and a Jacobean fireplace; there's also a very fine flint dovecote in its grounds. Now retrace your steps down Hangleton Lane but shortly turn left along a signed cycle path through Benfield Valley with its fine variety of plant life including meadow vetchling, red fescue, maple and blackthorn, and you should also look out for badgers and butterflies. Continue to a signed junction, bear right along a cycle path signed for Portslade, pass under the main road and climb up to Sharpthorne Crescent, crossing straight over onto a much narrower path to reach Mill Lane. Bear right into Mill Lane, immediately passing a useful bakery/café, and reaching a T-junction; bear left then immediately right along Mill Lane, but very shortly turn left onto a path which descends gently to reach a small green. As you reach it, turn left onto a path which enters Easthill Park, and bear half-right to arrive and follow a concrete path through the park. Your route follows the sign for the wild flower area but it's worth lingering in the park and detouring to inspect the lovely war memorial garden and the imposing Easthill House. Then join the signed path for the wild flower area, and forward out of the park down Park Close to a T-junction with Highlands Road. Turn left to follow it to a T-junction with Foredown Drive, then right to arrive back at the A270. Cross the road using the pedestrian crossing, and join a path which follows the left-hand edge of Victoria Recreation Ground you traversed earlier. Arriving at a T-junction with Victoria Road, turn left to retrace your steps to the station.

Preston Park *(Line E, 4.5 miles, linear walk to Brighton: moderate)*

Take the south exit from the station, walking down Clermont Road to the A23 Preston Road, crossing with care and turning right to follow it, bearing third left into Preston Drove. A short way up on the right are adjacent driveways, one leading to Preston Manor and the next to St Peter's church just above it; both are well worth visiting so check opening times carefully. The flint church of Early English origin is notable for its wall paintings, while Preston Manor, built in 1738, was once the manor house of a village outside Brighton. It's now a museum and evocation of Edwardian life, and supposedly one of Britain's most haunted houses, with evening ghost tours advertised. Go back down Preston Drove and left into Preston Road, soon bearing left to enter the green expanse of Preston Park itself. You immediately pass the so-called Preston Twins, a pair of elms 400 years old and possibly the oldest surviving English elms in the world, and follow the left edge of the park to reach the gateway to the gardens. Then return to Preston Road and walk back to Preston Drove, crossing Preston Road and turning left to pass the splendid grey tile-hung no 199, home of the Guerrand Hermes Foundation for Peace. Turn right into South Road and follow it past some excellent flint houses and then uphill under the railway, going forward into The Drove, rising very steeply. Go straight over the crossroads junction with Dyke Road into The Droveway and now descend, westwards, crossing Shirley Drive and Goldstone Crescent to enter Hove Park, opened in 1906. Keep straight on along the path through the park in the same direction, going forward to a continuation of The Droveway, now a metalled road again, rising to reach on the right what is a huge Victorian water-pumping station with 100ft brick chimney stack, preserved as the British Engineerium. Retrace your steps briefly into the park then as the road peters out to become a path again, just beyond the fence on the right, fork right along a narrow path, bearing right onto a wider path southwards down the west side of the park. There's a café to the left and Park View Road to the right. As the path reaches its south-westward end, watch out on the right for the so-called Gold Stone, thought to be a place of Druidic worship though only placed in its present spot when Hove Park opened.

Follow the path round and head northwards along the east side of the park then just before the children's play area bear right to rise to reach Goldstone Crescent, bearing left onto it briefly then right up Hove Park Road. You rise, and are able for a time to walk in another area of park just to the right, then cross over Shirley Drive and veer slightly left to reach Dyke Road again. Bear right to head downhill with Dyke Road, in a few hundred yards reaching the Booth Museum on the left. This is a remarkable natural history museum containing dinosaur bones, fossils, minerals and skeletons and stuffed birds in re-creations of their natural habitats. Cross over Dyke Road and walk a little further down to reach a café/toilet block, passing just to the nearside to reach a viewing platform for the lovely Dyke Road gardens. Turn right along a path which shortly veers left and heads for an open field; proceed to its bottom end, picking up a dirt track which immediately goes forward to reach a tennis court. Bear left to follow it round, veering right with it, then at its south-east corner veer right, downhill, across the playing field to its bottom (south-west) corner, crossing straight over Old Shoreham Road into Silverdale Road. Follow this to the end, turning right into Lyndhurst Road and almost immediately left into Lyndhurst Corner. Cross the railway, going forward into Holland Road, then at the crossroads junction with Cromwell Road/Davigdor Road turn left, next right into Somerhill Road and next left into Nizells Avenue. Opposite the plaque to Lord Alfred Douglas (on the left) turn right alongside the tennis court, now in St Ann's Well Park. At the T-junction of paths at the end turn left (by detouring right here you could visit the popular sensory garden, entered via an archway) and walk up towards the bowling club (through the trees to your right as you walk up is a charming lily pond and little cascade). Just before the bowling club turn right and ignoring crossing paths, walk up to St Ann's Well itself, the site of a now demolished pump house used to extract water recommended as a tonic by Dr Richard Russell, founder of modern Brighton. Turn left just before the well and head back to Nizells Avenue past a herb garden, choosing either the middle or right path at the triple-fork junction.

Turn right to continue up Nizells Avenue, crossing the York Avenue/Osmond Road crossroads into Windlesham Avenue, heading uphill to reach the B2122, noting the very attractive Vernon Terrace to the left. However you turn right into Denmark Terrace and then first left into Victoria Road, soon passing the 19th century St Michael's church which is to the left. The church has a magnificent Lady Chapel with chequerboard floor and white panelled ceiling, there's a superb window depicting the Flight Into Egypt, and there are massive Gothic arcades. Sadly it's only open on Saturdays and for services. Continue along Victoria Road to its end, going straight over into an alleyway which emerges onto Dyke Road. Cross over, turning right and almost immediately left to cut down through a small park, aiming for St Nicholas church, on the far side of Church Street. Turn left into Church Street, shortly reaching the church which is on the right; a flint building with a 14th century tower, it's actually Brighton's parish church. Continue down Church Street to reach a crossroads junction with Queens Road, turning left to follow it up to Brighton central station.

Pulborough *(Line A, 12 miles, circular walk: strenuous)*

Turn left out of station building into the car park, but just by the bike shed on the near right side, join a footpath which proceeds north-eastwards past an industrial estate to arrive at a T-junction with Church Place. Turn left to follow this road over the railway bridge – just beyond the bridge, look down the lane to your right to view the excellent Old Place, a former barn and now a house with much 15th and 16th century work – then continue along what is now Coombelands Lane. Shortly the road bends right with footpaths going off right and left; take the right-hand path which descends gently to cross a stream then veers left along a left-hand field edge, keeping the stream to the left. Follow the field edge briefly round to the right but then veer left as signed along the near side of the gallops to follow a track which brings you back beside Coombelands Lane. Now veer right to walk as signed parallel with the road (on the Wey South Path [WSP]) until you are directed back onto the road itself which you follow for just over half a mile to the hamlet of Pickhurst. Here turn left as signed (if you reach a road going off to the right, you've gone too far!) along a bridleway, still with the WSP, heading for Sheepwash, but in a couple of hundred yards veer right. Shortly you reach a path forking left; ignore this but continue on the WSP bridleway, soon reaching a path T-junction. Turn left here, westwards, to cross firstly the course of the Wey & Arun Junction Canal by the sturdy redbrick Pallingham Bridge, then the river Arun by another footbridge.

Shortly beyond this second footbridge the WSP veers sharply right, but you continue westwards on a signed footpath. Very shortly kink left as signed over a stream and right over a track, then continue in the same westerly direction along a right-hand field edge, woodland now dominating the scene ahead. Veer noticeably left with the field edge, and at the corner go straight ahead over the stile along a path through the wood. Go over a crossing track and very shortly reach a signed path junction, going straight on uphill and passing a delectable timber-framed cottage. You veer right to arrive at a signed path fork junction, forking right here along a right-hand field edge; you soon reach a path crossroads, going straight over but veering left across the field to follow the left-hand field edge to Springs Farm, reaching another signed path junction. Fork left here into the woods, going downhill and veering left to cross a lovely stream, then veering right to arrive at the lovely thatched Brinkwells, where a plate tells you Edward Elgar lived between 1917 and 1919. Continue on up the driveway then turn right onto the metalled lane and follow it to a post box by a slight right bend. Turn left here onto a signed footpath immediately to the left of the Warren Barn drive.

Follow the path through the woods, bearing right at a T-junction of paths to cross the drive then strike out north-westwards across a field to reach a signed T-junction of paths in the field. Turn right to follow the path (now on the Serpent Trail [ST]) across the field then down to another metalled road by Bedham Farm, turning left to follow it. There are lovely views through the trees and the road is extremely quiet so this is excellent walking. You pass the hamlet of Bedham and then veer sharply left; soon after this bend you reach a hairpin bend. Ignore signed footpaths diving away southwards off the bend itself but having swung round, turn left onto a bridleway which proceeds in a dead straight line just south of west through the woodlands of Flexham Park. The woodland path ends at a road junction (1). Here you have the option of shortening your walk by 4 miles by turning left into Riverhill Lane and following instructions from the asterisked point below; the full route however (which is retraced all the way back from (3) below) goes straight on along Kingspit Lane heading west then veering south-west downhill. As you descend look out for the ST sign directing you right along a wide track soon reaching a footpath sign (2), your route continuing straight on, north-westwards, from here. Some OS maps show the ST route continuing along the road for a couple of hundred yards then turning hard right along a signed path back uphill to reach

(2); the advantage of this longer route is that you get a fantastic view southwards towards the Downs from the hard right turn. However you have reached (2) now proceed north-westwards as signed along an excellent path, still on the ST, through the woods. In roughly half a mile from (2) you veer gently left (west) along a still excellent path, descending to cross a track with a hillside ahead. Signage and path definition here is poor, but you need to walk uphill across the pasture just left of the hilltop ahead of you, aiming in fact for a signboard warning you to keep dogs under control. You then will see a track through the pasture, going forward to join it and turn right onto it, passing another mini-summit which is just to your left and descending to a gate. Enjoying tremendous views to Petworth ahead, walk downhill along what is a clear path, but then look out clearly for and follow a signed path forking left (3), aiming for a footpath sign on the valley bottom by a stream crossing. It's now a clear path which then takes you steeply uphill to arrive at the bottom of a rough road onto which you turn right, climbing and passing the RC church, turning right into Angel Street, now in Petworth.

You pass the early 18th century Angel Hotel, bearing left into Middle Street and then right into High Street, though detouring left to visit the Cottage Museum, providing a fascinating insight into cottage life in the early years of the last

The very un-English tower of Petworth church

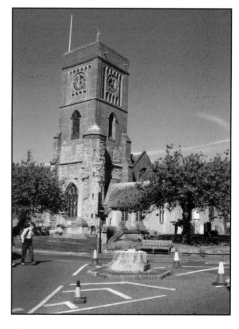

century. Then follow the High Street downhill to Golden Square, detouring left to visit the delightful courtyard including the excellent bookshop. Follow Golden Square on and turn left into Daymer's Bridge, then right and immediately right again into Market Square, turning left past the late 18th century Leconfield Hall and aiming just to the right of the newsagents at the top of the square along the very picturesque Lombard Street to reach the church which boasts a very un-English redbrick tower, 13th century chancel and several very fine memorials. Use the church path to cut round into North Street, heading northwards along it briefly then turning left as signed into the Petworth House complex. Walk down as signed to the tunnel entrance to Petworth Park, turning left through the tunnel, rising beyond the tunnel and turning left to reach Petworth House. Although it dates back six centuries, extensive rebuilding took place in the late 17th century, and today it's particularly noteworthy for its superb collection of paintings and sculpture work. The grounds and Petworth Park itself, which you may wish to detour to explore, were landscaped by Capability Brown in the mid-18th century. Retrace your steps to North Street, turn right and now follow it southwards to Barton Lane. Your way is left along this lane but to see a little more of Petworth carry on to the sharp right bend, turning left into East Street, following it to its end and turning right down New Street to reach Market Square, then returning to Barton Lane via Lombard Street and then right along the near side of North Street.

Follow Barton Lane which soon veers left and goes forward to a footpath which you follow straight ahead, steeply downhill, then continue uphill and along a left-hand field edge to reach point (3) above, retracing your steps all the way to point (1) above. This time, however, turn right down Riverhill Lane* which you follow south-eastwards for roughly half a mile, enjoying sensational views throughout. As the road bends right near its end, bear left onto a signed path which brings you to another road; cross straight over and join a well-signed path which heads fractionally east of south then southwards, downhill, veering left near the end to reach another road and the beautiful hamlet of Little Bognor. Turn right to follow the road past the buildings, then in a couple of hundred yards turn left onto a signed path, soon forking right, downhill, then veering right at the bottom to follow a right-hand field edge just west of south. You reach a T-junction of paths and now turn left, south-east, across the field, aiming initially for a path sign you can see in the middle of the field 100 yards or so ahead, then veering very gently left, aiming for the woods. As you approach the woods the entry into them and then the path through them becomes clear. You soon reach a field and veer gently right across the field then at the next boundary veer left to arrive at Bedham Lane, now in Fittleworth, opposite a delectable timber-framed cottage. Turn right to arrive shortly at the A283.

Cross with great care, turn right then bear immediately left, signed for the church. If you were in a hurry you could follow this road down to the B2138, possibly detouring to visit the church with medieval bells, Early English tower and chancel and 14th century octagonal font. You would then turn left (south-eastwards) onto the B2138 to proceed. However the recommended route turns almost immediately right off the road along a signed path through the trees, keeping the A283 just to the right. Pass just to the right of the scout hut and arrive at a road, bearing right then immediately left into the Hesworth Common car park. Follow straight through the car park onto a clear path then at the first crossroads turn right, following a path up steps to reach a trig point and breathtaking views to the Downs. Return to the crossroads, going straight over; at the next crossroads, turn left, then bear right at the next T-junction, arriving at the top of a lane. Turn left, down the lane, to arrive at the B2138, turning right (south-eastwards) to follow this road.

Having joined the B2138, bear left very shortly along a signed footpath, soon crossing straight over a road then kinking right at a fork of routes. From here proceed eastwards along the northern (left-hand) edge of Fittleworth Common, avoiding right forks into the woods and veering left to arrive back at the A283, crossing straight over. Join a path forking right, north-eastwards, initially not terribly clear but then proceeding to a path junction and bearing right as signed. Follow what is now an excellent path heading eastwards then just south of east, going forward to become a road, being joined by another road coming from the right. Very shortly after that you reach a T-junction, enjoying an excellent view to the stone-built Stopham Manor House ahead, arriving in the village of Stopham. Turn right onto the road, which veers right (it's worth detouring to the lovely Norman church to the left here) and heads just west of south to reach the A283.

Turn left to follow the A283 briefly – thankfully there is a pavement – passing the late 18th century Stopham House which is on the right, then in a couple of hundred yards fork right to cross the beautiful Stopham Bridge, dating back to 1423, and reach the beautifully-sited adjacent pub. Turn left by the pub up a signed footpath which must be one of the shortest in Sussex, bringing you back to the A283. Cross over it for the last time, straight onto a signed bridleway, back with the WSP. Follow it along the south-east edge of woodland, enjoying magnificent views across the Arun valley towards the Downs; as you get within sight of the end of the woods, look out for the Park Mound motte and bailey which is to the left, an extraordinary natural "hump" in the woodland. Emerge from the woods and continue in roughly the same direction to cross a lane just north of Park Farm, then follow a clear signed path downhill, veering left to arrive back at Coombelands Lane. Turn right to follow it, soon crossing the railway, then shortly bear right down the footpath returning you to Pulborough station.

Robertsbridge *(Line H, 8 miles, circular walk: moderate)*
Exit the station onto Station Road (the headquarters of the Rother Valley Railway, devoted to preserving the Robertsbridge end of the defunct Robertsbridge-Headcorn railway, can be accessed across the station car park) turning left to

follow it eastwards to a T-junction with High Street. This is one of the most picturesque village streets in Sussex; between the George Inn at the top, and the Seven Stars further down, there are many superb brick and timbered houses. The continuous route turns left onto the High Street then shortly right into Fair Lane, following it to the A21, bearing right to cross the road by a footbridge, dropping down to a continuation of Fair Lane and turning right to follow it. Continue eastwards along the lane past the buildings of Redlands and about a mile from Robertsbridge you reach a sharp right bend in the lane by a house which is to the left. In the grounds of this house are the ruins of a Cistercian abbey which was founded towards the end of the 12th century; they are visible from the lane but not open to the public. Just beyond the right bend is a sharp left bend and a little beyond that you reach a path junction, a bridleway going off to the right. However you continue eastwards along a path, leaving the security of the lane and now following pasture as signposted. Your well-signed path veers gently right then left, keeping the still quite narrow river Rother to your left, but just as you get into your stride you reach a signed footpath going off to the left; if you find yourself confronted with a sign pointing you sharp right, you've gone too far! Your left turn crosses a channel and immediately veers right to become a narrow and delightful path through the trees between the channel which is to your right, and the Rother which is to your left. When the Rother veers sharply left to pass under the course of the old Rother Valley railway, your path continues on eastwards, following a clear course across fields aiming for Junction Road ahead. Go straight on through the vegetation on a clear path to arrive at the road.

Turn left to follow the road very briefly, then turn right along what feels like a very private driveway heading for Udiam. However shortly you're reassured by a path forking right just beyond the trees arriving at a field. Walk steeply uphill through the fields aiming just to the right of the buildings at the top, then on reaching a track at the top turn left to walk past the buildings downhill. Beyond the buildings the track bends sharply left, but you turn hard right here, walking just south of east, aiming for trees ahead. A sign clearly directs you immediately to the right of the trees, descending steeply to enter the woods at the bottom left corner of the field; you then climb again, veering south-east along an obvious path to bring you to a metalled minor road. Turn left to follow this road, soon veering right and descending to reach Bodiam station. This is, at the time of writing, the terminus of another section of the former Robertsbridge-Headcorn railway known as the Kent & East Sussex Railway, providing steam train rides between Bodiam and Tenterden in Kent.

Walk on beyond the station to shortly cross the wider Rother at Bodiam Bridge and arrive at the entrance to Bodiam Castle which is to the right. Ideally you should do this walk when the castle is open, but even if it isn't, you should still be able to access the castle grounds. Make your

The majestic and photogenic Bodiam Castle

way to the castle and pass round to its left side, effectively following round it in an anti-clockwise direction to reach the bridge over the moat into the castle itself. Arguably the finest and most photogenic castle in Sussex, it was built in 1385 as a response to fears of French invasion; it was badly damaged in the English Civil War but was restored at the end of the 19th century and a number of fine features remain including gatehouse with portcullis, great hall, servants' hall, kitchen and chapel. For a great view of the castle and the Rother valley from above, walk the short distance from here to the top north-eastern corner of the grounds, going over a stile to follow the Sussex Border Path uphill, fractionally west of north on a left-hand field edge to the top of the hill. The view is possibly the highlight of the whole walk. Whether you've detoured or not, retrace your steps past the castle café to the main castle entrance/exit.

Turn right to follow the road very briefly, then turn left just beyond the pub onto a signed path heading westwards along a lane. It's very straightforward going, the lane veering gently left then gently right, then left to proceed westwards to arrive at the edge of a small industrial estate with a map on a notice-board. Do NOT take the signed "conservation walk" to the right of the estate; instead follow the road into the estate, then just beyond the buildings veer left, south-westwards, as clearly signed. There is momentarily the feeling of encroaching in a large private garden, but soon you see and follow a clear track continuing south-westwards, before veering right, just south of west, to reach Junction Road once more.

Cross the road and immediately veer left as signed, then just before the field boundary at the top, veer right across the field, going forward into the next field. You proceed fractionally south of west across the field, keeping ponds, shrouded in patches of woodland, to the left; this is lovely hilltop walking with beautiful views. You reach a line of trees at a field boundary, going over into the next field. Don't be tempted to go straight on – you'll reach a dead end – but veer very gently right across this next field to the top right corner of the field just south of Mayfield Farm. Pass into the next field, following close to the left-hand edge, continuing westwards, noting further ponds in the trees to the left. You shortly arrive at Bourne Lane, turning left along it and soon veering sharp right to continue in a westerly direction; stay on it until a junction with Rocks Hill, turning left onto it and descending to Salehurst, enjoying excellent views to the right. As you reach the buildings of the village, bear left into Beech House Lane to almost immediately arrive by the church and Salehurst Halt pub. The church is particularly noteworthy for its font with a 13th century base, and its tower dates back to the 14th century. Turn sharp right by the church into Church Road which proceeds pleasantly through the Rother valley to reach a roundabout junction with the A21. Cross over the A21 into Northbridge Street (road) using the right-hand side of the roundabout – there is a pedestrian crossing to the right for a safer crossing – then follow Northbridge Street round to the left, going forward into The Clappers. Continue on into the High Street, turning right into Station Road and following it back to the station.

Rye *(Line C, 1.5 miles, circular walk: easy)*

From the station exit make your way straight up Station Approach, over Cinque Ports Street and up Market Road, turning right into the High Street which swings to the left and becomes the Mint. At the junction of the Mint and Mermaid Street turn right and walk down towards the waterfront, shortly reaching the Rye Heritage Centre which is immediately to your right; it includes an amazing depiction of how Rye was in 1872 with lighting and commentary. Cross over the main road, South Undercliff, and bear right, then shortly left round a barrier to access the quay, turning left to follow the waterfront downstream. At the exit by the left bend of the road, leave the quay and cross the road, going over into Strand, with its restored black-painted wooden warehouses, following it to arrive back at the bottom of cobbled Mermaid Street. Now turn right to follow it uphill, passing the timber-framed early 16th century Mermaid Inn, and at the top, turn right into West Street, shortly reaching the 18th century redbrick Lamb House which is to your right. It is best known for its association with the novelists E F Benson and Henry James who both lived here, Benson being the author of the Mapp &

Lucia books, set in and around Rye. Follow West Street to Church Square and turn immediately right to reach the top end of Watchbell Street, turning right again to walk down this beautiful street and enjoying an excellent view from its bottom end by the Hope Anchor Inn. Follow Watchbell Street back to Church Square and go

Mermaid Street, one of Rye's loveliest streets

straight on to the far (north-eastern) end, bearing right to reach Rye Castle, also known as Ypres Tower. Built in 1249, it's one of Rye's oldest buildings, being built as the castle of Rye but subsequently becoming a prison. There's a museum within the tower, and beyond it in Gun Garden there's a platform with a display of cannons and cannonballs, and excellent views towards the sea.

Now walk along the east side of the square to a T-junction with Market Street, turning right and walking past the 15th century timber-framed Flushing Inn. Veer left down East Street, passing another museum which is to the left; this includes a wide range of attractions, from a 1745 fire engine to a Captain Pugwash treasure hunt (John Ryan, writer of the Pugwash books, made his home in Rye). At the end, turn right into the High Street and follow it briefly as far as telescope and splendid viewpoint, continuing along the street to reach the 14th century Landgate, the last remaining one of Rye's original medieval gates. Walk back along the High Street until you come to Lion Street which is to the left, while to your right here is the Old Grammar School dating back to 1636 with distinctive Dutch gables. Turn left by the George Inn up Lion Street, now heading for the church; on the right, just before you reach the church, is Simon the Pieman tearoom and the 15th century timber-framed Fletcher's House, the birthplace of the dramatist John Fletcher in 1579, while to the left, pretty much opposite the tearoom, is the fine arcaded 18th century Town Hall. The Norman church of St Mary, immediately beyond, is particularly famous for its 16th century clock, the oldest working church turret clock in the country. Turn right (as you look towards the church entrance) immediately before the church along a pedestrian passage past the lovely pink-painted Old Vicarage and cottages with lovely gardens, arriving back at West Street; follow it back to Lamb House, veering right and walking back to the High Street. Turn right to follow it to the junction with Lion Street, crossing over and now doubling back along the south side of the High Street past the superb Martello Bookshop with a particularly good range of books by local authors. Shortly turn right into Market Road and walk straight on from there to the station.

St Leonards Warrior Square *(Lines C & H, 1.5 miles, linear walk to Hastings: easy)*

Exit the station on the westbound platform side, going straight on into Western Road. Take the second left turning into Terrace Road, and go first right into Warrior Square, enjoying views across beautiful gardens to gracious houses on each side. Turn left into the gardens and take the steps downhill then follow diagonally to the bottom left corner. Cross over the road then walk down to enter the lower section of garden on the other side, bearing right then left and right again to reach the bottom right corner, now meeting the A259 coast road. Don't cross the road but turn left to arrive at the splendid memorial to Queen Victoria – then cross the coast road and follow it eastwards to some steps, climbing these to reach and follow the promenade. Carry on all the way to the pier, here crossing the road to admire the White Rock Theatre, then following the immediately adjacent Schwerte Way and bearing left from there up St Margaret's Road and right into Falaise Road. Almost immediately though bear right to walk parallel with Falaise Road but through White Rock Gardens. You arrive at the top end, at the junction of Falaise Road and the A21, crossing over with care to visit the Hastings Museum and Art Gallery. This includes the Durbar Hall, featuring collections of artefacts from the far East, and there are also exhibits relating to John Logie Baird, the inventor of television, and the architect James Burton.

The White Rock Theatre adjacent to Hastings pier

Cross back over the road and re-enter White Rock

Gardens but this time go straight on, following the path along the top of the gardens roughly parallel with the A21, veering right to arrive at a T-junction with a driveway onto which you turn left to exit the gardens. Turn right into White Rock Road, then shortly left into the road called White Rock Gardens, following it to its end and bearing left into Prospect Place to return to the A21; bear right to follow it briefly then right again down Brassey Steps to reach the church of Holy Trinity. You're now in the so-called America Ground area of Hastings, so-called because following a dispute as to land ownership a group of residents tried to claim this area as an American state in the early 19th century. I suggest you bear left into Trinity Street (where you can access the church if it's open) then shortly hard right into Robertson Street; both these streets plus Claremont, making up the triangle, contain some interesting and individual shops and businesses. Then from Robertson Street return to the seafront and bear left to continue along the concrete promenade, clearly signed as a cycleway/walkway which veers noticeably right. As you get level with a blue beach hut which is to your right and toilets to your left, bear left (signposted toilets), passing the end of the crazy golf course and walking on to the coast road (A259). Cross it in front of the De Luxe entertainment complex and turn left, then almost immediately turn right up a flight of steps bringing you to Pelham Crescent. Walk along it, passing the Pantheon-like church of St Mary in the Castle, built in 1828, boasting four splendid Ionic columns. Walk on down Pelham Crescent, turn right and follow the inland side of the coast road, bearing right at Breeds Place into the main shopping area, passing underneath Albert Road using a pedestrian underpass. This brings you to Wellington Place and the main shopping centre in Hastings. Simply then turn right as signed into Havelock Road and walk uphill to arrive at Hastings station.

Seaford *(Line D, 11 miles, linear walk to Eastbourne: strenuous)*

Turn right out of the station and immediately reach a busy road junction, bearing right into Church Street, with the church of St Leonard in front of you. Walk down Church Street, veering left into South Street (don't continue southwards down Church Street which is effectively a turning off) and passing the Old Town Hall, then at a crossroads junction, with the High Street going off to the left, turn right, passing the lovely Wellington Hotel. Go straight over Steyne Road into the Causeway and follow it, crossing the Esplanade and turning left to follow the promenade to its end, past the Martello tower of 1810, the most westerly of these defensive towers built during the Napoleonic Wars. Having passed it, or possibly viewed the museum housed inside it, go forward to the car park at the end of the promenade.

Now begin a steady climb up onto the cliffs of Seaford Head, keeping the cliff edge to the right (take care not to get too close) and the golf course to your left. It's never intolerably steep, but it's hard going, so pause lots and enjoy the increasingly good views back to Seaford and Newhaven. Eventually you make it onto Seaford Head, the site of a triangular Iron Age hillfort, and of great interest to the naturalist and geologist; plants hereabouts include thrift, ground ivy and kidney vetch, and the area is also popular with rabbits. Continue along the clifftop enjoying superb views to the Seven Sisters cliffs ahead of you. All too soon, it seems, you begin to descend on a magnificent green path, but you should detour down steps to the fossil-rich shore at Hope Gap with its splendid cliff faces and rocky pavements, legacy of a Late Cretaceous marine environment some 89 million years ago.

Now veering half-left, you rise again to get an excellent view of Cuckmere Haven, the valley between Seaford Head and the Seven Sisters through which the estuary of the Cuckmere River flows. Remaining on the cliff path you reach the coastguard cottages; pass to the left of them and turn right onto a clear track beside the cottages, descending to the Cuckmere valley bottom, known as Cuckmere Haven. You arrive at a gate, but rather than bearing left here as suggested by the Vanguard Way arrow, go straight through the gate onto the shingle beach, and forward to the west bank of Cuckmere estuary itself, just as it arrives at the sea. This totally unspoilt valley is the only one in Sussex to provide wildfowl with a natural merging of meadowmarsh, saltings and a wild seashore, and boasts a huge variety of bird life including cormorants, herons, dabchicks, curlews, peregrine falcons, hen harriers and Canada geese. Turn left to join a narrow but clear path up the west bank of the estuary, a new cut of the Cuckmere; the path kinks left away from the water, then veers right and goes forward to the A259 at the Golden Galleon pub. Turn right onto this road and immediately cross the footbridge over the Cuckmere – there is a pavement on the far side – and carry on beside this busy road as far as the visitor centre and adjacent café at Exceat a few hundred yards along the road.

More or less opposite the visitor centre, the road bends left and begins to ascend, and you follow the road briefly to the bus stop (1). If you were pushed for time here, you could continue your journey by turning right through a gate onto an excellent track heading seawards. However, the recommended route crosses the road here and heads north-eastwards along the South Downs Way (SDW) as signed, walking steeply up a grassy hillside to reach a stone stile, pausing to enjoy a quite fantastic view across the Cuckmere valley. Cross the stile and enter woodland, walking down a long flight of steps to reach the delightful village of Westdean, in an exquisite wooded valley setting. Go forward onto a metalled road with a high wall to your right, veering right with the road and passing the lovely Old Parsonage and Norman church of All Saints which are to your left; looking to the right you'll see the site of a palace of Alfred the Great and you can see ruins of a medieval manor house and in the far left corner, a medieval dovecote. Continue to

The Seven Sisters, climax of the South Downs Way

follow the road round to the right (the Manor House just in sight ahead on this right turn) passing further beautiful flint houses both to the right and left, then bear right again. You pass the dovecote which is just over the wall, and keeping the wall to your right, continue round to complete the circle. Simply now retrace yoiur steps up through the wood, over the stone stile and back down the grassy hillside, crossing the A259 to get back to point (1) above. Now pass through the gate onto the excellent track referred to above and follow it back towards the sea, admiring the extraordinary meanders of the "old" Cuckmere estuary to your right.

After roughly half a mile the path swings quite sharply left away from the valley, towards a group of farm buildings; don't swing left with it, but fork right onto a path signposted Seven Sisters, pass through a gate, then after about 100 yards fork left. You're now on the course of the SDW. Initially your path remains on the flat but then proceeds up a flight of steps, going forward to a fence; don't cross the gate in the fence that soon appears, but keeping the fence to your right, press on uphill along a clearly marked path. This is quite a slog, mitigated by the increasingly great views, but at length you arrive at the summit of the first of seven spectacular chalk clifftops known as the Seven Sisters. The Seven Sisters, seven spectacular chalk cliffs, form the eastern end of the South Downs and the climax of the SDW, and owe their origin to geological activity between 50 and 100 million years ago.

Now the going could not be more straightforward, albeit it's hard work! There's no path as such: just take each "sister" in turn, enjoying the quite magnificent views back to Seaford Head and Cuckmere Haven, and forward towards the Belle Tout lighthouse and Beachy Head. The climbs are often steep and you need to be careful not to stray too close to the cliff edge as you ascend. The seventh "sister" having been conquered, you descend towards the assembly of houses at Birling Gap, taking care, as you come down off the final "sister," to veer a little left to a gate in the fence beyond which it's a straightforward walk down to the houses. There's also a café here and a chance to recuperate. Lying at the eastern end of the Seven Sisters, Birling Gap is a freak cleft in the South Downs with steep steps to the sea that were used by smugglers, and you should pause to note the row of houses here and how exposed they are to the sea.

Beyond the Gap, the way forward is obvious, with a choice of paths to take you back up to and along the clifftops, aiming for and passing to the left of the old (19th century) granite Belle Tout lighthouse. It proved somewhat ineffective in the thick sea mists and a 125ft high sea level lighthouse below the Beachy Head clifftop was built to replace the Belle Tout in 1902. You need to pass to the left of the lighthouse as signed, then drop steeply to meet the road at a small car park, before beginning the assault on Beachy Head. It's a laborious climb, not helped by a big dip which sees you rapidly lose height you must then regain, but at least route-finding is no problem, the grass is lovely to walk on, and the views just get better and better. Finally you arrive on Beachy Head, well over 500ft above the sea, the highest point and the best viewpoint being situated at the round redbrick-surrounded seating area. The name Beachy Head is thought to derive from the Middle Ages French "beau chef" meaning "beautiful headland" and on a clear day it offers views which on a clear day can extend back to the Isle of Wight and even as far as France. Since 1990 it has become a breeding ground for falcons, it is one of the best places in Sussex to see the stone curlew, and plants include red valerian, sea radish, early gentian, harebell and orchid.

From the seating area described above, and using the trig point straight ahead as a marker, go forward to a metalled crossing path pretty much level with the Beachy Head pub (which of course you may wish to patronise, and also detour to the trig point, before proceeding!). Turn right (seawards) onto the metalled path which, as it reaches the cliff edge, describes an extravagant loop. Take the short cut across the loop using the (SDW-signed) path provided, and suddenly a fantastic view to Eastbourne and Hastings opens out ahead. Go straight over onto a path which is seen to contour the hillside, but having joined it, turn right immediately(by the SDW sign) onto a path which heads exceedingly steeply downhill, aiming for the cliff edge. Take great care! At length you reach the cliff edge, then veer left to walk along the cliff top, continuing through vegetation, ironically having to climb up some steps and then climbing again to meet a wide stony track. Turn right onto this track which becomes a metalled road and drops down to a café, just beyond which you turn right into Duke's Drive and follow it downhill. You pass the Helen Gardens then immediately beyond them turn right along a narrow road signposted Holywell, Promenade (Western Parade); keep along this road downhill, ignoring turnings off, to arrive at the promenade, then turn left and follow the promenade all the way to Eastbourne, a walk of about a mile. Stick to the lower promenade then just beyond the bandstand, a little way short of the pier, climb onto the upper promenade beside the coast road. Turn left into Terminus Road which you follow to the town centre; at the T-junction at the end, turn left to pass the Arndale centre and arrive at the railway station.

Shoreham-by-Sea *(Line B, 14 miles, circular walk: strenuous)*

From the north platform of Shoreham station (for trains for Brighton and London) exit onto Brunswick Road and cross straight over into Queen's Place opposite. Follow this road to a crossroads junction, going straight over into Hebe Road and following this to its junction with Victoria Road. Cross straight over into Swiss Gardens and then turn first left into Freehold Street, taking you to a T-junction with Old Shoreham Road. Turn right into this road, cross over, and follow the road north-westwards, passing a row of houses, beyond which you turn very shortly left to join the Downs Link (DL) footpath. This footpath, as its name implies, links the South Downs and North Downs, and for much of its course overlaps with the course of the defunct Shoreham-Christ's Hospital railway line. Immediately to your left is the Adur estuary, with views across to the magnificent Lancing College chapel (which you'll visit later in this walk), while ahead of you is the A27 flyover. A little way before the flyover you get level with a footbridge over the Adur; you could detour right off the path here, crossing the main road to visit the church of St Nicholas, Old Shoreham, much restored but with Saxon and Norman features. There are particularly impressive Norman arch carvings, and the 13th century wooden screen across the chancel is one of the oldest in England. Whether you detour here or not, you continue beside the Adur upstream, and I suggest that at this point you switch from the DL to a good parallel path along the river bank, providing a much better view to the river. Then having passed under the flyover, shortly before the river bends left, make your way down the bank to rejoin the DL.

Continue on now through pleasant but unspectacular countryside to the old Beeding cement works, arriving at the river again and following its right bank upstream, then in just under half a mile or so cross the river by the bridge. Beyond the bridge walk briefly along the left bank but soon arrive at a junction of paths, where you turn left to follow the South Downs Way away from the river. You arrive at a junction of paths, forking right along the DL, but by detouring left to the road and turning left again you very shortly reach the picturesque church of Botolphs, wonderfully unspoilt, containing some late Saxon features including wall-paintings and a splendid Jacobean pulpit. Whether you've detoured or not, keep on now along the DL, turning left at a signed path junction to follow it as far as the A283; cross with great care and continue on an obvious path on the other side, parallel with the A283, soon reaching a roundabout. Sticking to the DL, take the road between the A283 and the Street, Castle Lane, which runs immediately to the right (east) of the A283, and parallel with it. You then go straight on into Roman Road, following it to a T-junction, here turning left along King's Barn Lane. Cross over the A283 then follow the road, now Jarvis Lane, veering right with the road which now becomes Cripps Lane, then continue downhill into Church Street, following it into lovely Steyning. You soon pass the parish church of St Andrew, which boasts a late Norman nave with arcades and clerestories, completed by the end of the 12th century and decorated with quite magnificent Norman carvings depicting the heads of both humans and animals. In the 16th century was added the west tower and the reredos of 48 carved panels, one of which bears the coat of arms of Henry VIII. Further up is the old Grammar School, founded in 1614 but housed in a 15th century building known as the Brotherhood Hall. At the end of Church Street you reach a mini-roundabout, now in the town centre; your continuous route bears left into the High Street, but you really should turn right onto the High Street to enjoy the town centre, dominated by the tile-hung Old Market House and its very prominent clock tower. There are several examples of 14th and 15th century hall houses, with the Post Office being one of the best. Many of the building use a laminated sandstone called Horsham stone for roof covering, but there are plenty of other building styles evident in the town, including tile-hanging, timber-framing and weather-boarding.

Now walk along the High Street downhill from the mini-roundabout away from the centre. Remain on the same road, ignoring turnings-off; the road veers to the right and rises, then levels out, veers left and drops to a roundabout junction with the A283. Cross it on its left side, turning left into Castle Road then immediately bear hard right up along a metalled road, through a parking area and up steps to reach the impressive castle ruins. The castle was built soon after the Norman invasion and during the Middle Ages saw many important visitors including King John in 1216, and Edward I between 1285 and 1302. The castle was all but destroyed by the Parliamentary army during the English Civil War and only a fragment of it now survives. Go back down the steps but now veer left to pass (or visit) the adjacent Norman church of St Nicholas, and drop down to The Street, following it on in the same direction through the village of Bramber. A little further on along The Street on the right-hand side is St Mary's House, a superb timber-framed house dating back to around 1470. It boasts a number of

One of the few surviving parts of Bramber Castle

fine rooms, including the Monk's Parlour, notable for its huge "dragon" beam and 17th century inglenook; the Hall, embellished with beautiful 17th century gilded wall-leather; the Octagonal Dining Room displaying over 80 costume dolls; the Painted Room, with its fascinating "trompe l'oeil" murals said to have been painted for a visit by Elizabeth I; and the Library, containing a unique private collection of works by the Victorian comic poet Thomas Hood.

A little further beyond St Mary's turn right just before Beeding Bridge to join the right bank of the Adur which you'll follow most of the way back to Shoreham. The first landmark, just a short riverside walk away, is the bridge carrying the A283 over the river. Beyond the bridge, the surroundings become slightly marred by the main road and old cement works, but there are good views to the Downs in either direction, as well as the church at Botolphs you may have visited earlier. You pass the footbridge you crossed previously, continuing to follow the right bank downstream; immediately to your right are flat fields but beyond them is a rolling downland landscape with the ground rising to over 400 feet. Lancing College Chapel now dominates the view immediately ahead and the views are delightful, especially to Mill Hill on your left. Now the A27 flyover comes into view, but it's a little further away than you think, as you need to leave the bank of the Adur to negotiate a tributary channel; you walk beside this channel as far as a parking area beside the metalled Coombes Road at Cuckoo Corner.

The next two miles consist of a detour to Lancing College Chapel and back. If you wish to press on along the continuous walking route, don't join the road but walk very briefly through the car park and bear left along the far side of the tributary channel to regain the right bank of the Adur. To make the detour, turn left on to the road at Cuckoo Corner and follow it for about half a mile, then bear right as signposted onto the road signposted for Lancing College. Shortly you reach a junction and fork right as signed for the college. However, almost immediately beyond the right fork, you see a stile on the right, and you need to cross this stile and follow the signed public footpath (not the signed bridleway) through the meadow, following the direction shown by the signpost. It's a lovely walk through the meadows, and you may see horses and rabbits here. Aim to the left of the thick patch of trees along a clear path which rises to reach a road onto which you turn right and which you follow uphill to the junction at the top, turning left to shortly arrive at the chapel. Begun in 1868, it was built in early 14th century English Gothic style using Sussex sandstone and its foundations are in places seventy feet deep. With an internal height of 94ft it is the fourth highest church interior in England. Its outstanding features are its painted ceiling, the comparatively recent (1978) stained glass Rose Window at its west end, and the massive tapestries above the High Altar, woven in 1933 and at one time the biggest in the country. You'll then need to retrace your steps to Cuckoo Corner the same way. On arriving at the car park, bear right along the south side of the tributary channel to arrive back at the right bank of the Adur and resume the continuous walk.

Beyond Cuckoo Corner, it's now a straightforward walk along the right bank of the Adur towards then under the A27, and a short way beyond the flyover just short of the airfield adjoining Shoreham Airport, you reach the footbridge known as Old Shoreham Bridge. Turn left and cross over the bridge to join the left bank just by the church of St Nicholas. Turn right to retrace your steps along the DL but this time keep walking along the river bank beyond the point at which you joined it, going under the railway bridge and on to the top of a slipway with Little High Street going off to your left. Turn left to follow Little High Street, going forward into Shoreham High Street itself. You pass the impressive 19th century Town Hall which is on the right, now a pub/bar, and on the left is Marlipins, an unusual example of a surviving secular non-military Norman building with an exterior that is made of very distinctive chequerboard flint and Caen stone; once a customs house, it is now a museum containing historic ship models and relics of local history.

Continue briefly along the High Street then turn left up Church Street. This is Shoreham's loveliest street, with several lovely flint-fronted buildings, including, on the right-hand side, one in which Captain Henry Roberts lived in the 18th century; a plate tells you that he explored the South Seas with Captain Cook. Other highlights are Manor House, the flint-built Old Scantlings, Dolphin

Cottage which a sign indicates dates back to 1754, and the site of St Saviour's School founded here in 1858. Go straight on into the churchyard of the church of St Mary de Haura ("of the harbour"), Shoreham's principal place of worship, dating back to 1130. Despite losing its nave in 1720, it still boasts magnificent choirstalls and tower which at 81ft high is visible for miles. Whether or not you've visited the church, follow round to the far (north) side of it, along the main church path, arriving at St Mary's Road at its junction with the top end of East Street. There are some splendid buildings on the north side of St Mary's Road including the tile-hung St Mary's Cottage and also St Mary's House, described on a plate as the first school of the Society of St Mary, founded here in August 1848. Walk eastwards along St Mary's Road, turning shortly left into Brunswick Road, soon reaching Shoreham-by-Sea station on the right.

Southbourne *(Line A, 7 miles, linear walk to Nutbourne: moderate)*

From the railway station, walk southwards down Stein Road, very shortly turning right into First Avenue then left into The Drive, following it down to the A259. Cross with care, turn right and walk beside the A259 briefly then turn left along the road signed for Prinsted, appropriately enough Prinsted Lane; it intially heads southwards, veering south-westwards then southwards again at a junction in the village centre. Prinsted is a delightful and totally unspoilt village with some of the prettiest cottages on the Sussex coast. The oldest and most picturesque part of the village is round the junction referred to above, forming a tiny square, with cottages of flint and brick, several thatched, some timber-framed, within a short radius of the square; it's worth detouring up the road to the right and back to the square in order to see some of the cottages, before heading southwards to the shore. You reach a sharp right bend in the road where there's a car park and a small flight of steps up a bank which you climb to arrive at the embankment path beside Chichester Harbour, turning left to follow it. This is a quite delightful walk at any time of year; Chichester Harbour teems with a fine array of birds including wild swans, brent geese, shelducks, curlews, dunlins, sandwich terns, ringed plovers and oystercatchers, while plants include glasswort, sea lavender and sea purslane. The views are magnificent, both across to the Chidham peninsula and also back to Thorney Island. The going is extremely easy, the path metalled either wholly or partially, veering initially right (southwards) then left (eastwards) aiming for the far corner of the inlet and what is the start of the Chidham peninsula. A tide mill was built hereabouts towards the end of the 17th century, barges visiting to load and unload at the mill; the marshes are now designated as a local bird sanctuary and nature reserve.

A beautiful view across Chichester Harbour to Bosham

Now proceed along the coast path to begin your walk along the west side of the Chidham peninsula. The immediate area contains some of the earliest signs of human habitation that have been unearthed round the harbour, with recent excavations showing that man has been populating this part of the coast for 4000 years. You soon veer sharp right to reach Chidham Point then simply continue along the water's edge, enjoying lovely views across to Thorney Island. You arrive at a patch of trees where progress seems to be barred by a "private" sign, but a small flight of wooden steps enables you to join the shingle beach and follow this. You then reach another flight of steps which takes you back up to a proper path and, keeping Chichester Harbour to your right, you now go forward along a clear metalled waterside path, rounding Cobnor Point. Just across the water is the very popular sailing centre of Itchenor on the Manhood Peninsula.

You now swing north-eastwards, keeping Bosham Channel to your right and enjoying excellent views to Holy Trinity Church at Bosham. The signage directs you slightly away from the water as you pass the buildings of Cobnor and its Activities Centre, but you're soon reunited with the water's edge and proceed on to arrive at a lane known as Harbour Way, following this to arrive at Chidham Lane. You now (1) have a choice. You could turn right, almost immediately reaching an embankment which is on the right, with a lovely pool to your left, and you bear right to scramble up the embankment and join a path which continues along the waterside. Alternatively, if you want to see the village of Chidham, you could turn left at (1) and almost immediately right onto a footpath which, enjoying good views towards the Downs and Kingley Vale, heads westwards and passes a greenhouse to reach a junction of lanes. Go straight on into Cot Lane, soon veering left and then right to reach the pretty 13th century church. It contains a chapel dedicated to St Cuthman, it having been suggested that his journey to Steyning, pushing his mother in a wheelbarrow, began at Chidham. Continue along the road past a splendid flint barn as far as the popular brick-built Old House At Home pub. Having enjoyed a drink here, retrace your steps down Cot Lane, turning left at the junction into Steels Lane past the excellent red-brick Middleton House, and then right at the T-junction at the end into Chidham Lane, almost immediately bearing left up steps onto the embankment.

Now, whether you've detoured or not, continue on the embankment heading eastwards. It becomes very rough and overgrown and you do need to be careful where you're putting your feet; you could drop down to the left and follow a clear path running parallel with the embankment but with greatly restricted views, or you could do a bit of each, dropping down only when the going becomes too difficult. The views are sensationally good, not only to Bosham but to Kingley Vale Nature Reserve and on a clear day you can easily see the Trundle and its mast well to the north of Chichester. In due course the embankment diminishes and you go forward to a footbridge over a little stream and then a proper surfaced and raised path which takes you to the A259. Turn left to follow it, past the Bosham Inn which is to your right, soon turning right into Broad Road and following it to Nutbourne station.

Southease *(Line D, 7.5 miles, linear walk to Glynde: strenuous)*

Your continuous walk begins by your leaving Southease station and following the adjacent road eastwards towards the busy A26 along the South Downs Way (SDW). However, I recommend you begin by heading along the road westwards, over the Ouse, following the road all the way to the 12th century Southease church which contains Jacobean box pews and a fine 15th century chancel arch of wood, lath and plaster. Then return to the station the same way to begin the continuous route.

Follow the road eastwards from Southease station as stated, then turn right shortly as SDW-signed and soon left over the bridge across the A26; now following the clearly signed SDW, you swing southwards then north-eastwards onto Itford Hill, climbing all the while. You then veer eastwards, still ascending, and just over a mile from the A26 crossing you reach the Itford Hill trig point. It's worth detouring from the path to the trig point to enjoy the views which are sensational, particularly to the Ouse valley which you can follow with your eyes all the way from Lewes to the sea. Press on along the SDW; having reached the top of the escarpment you can enjoy easy progress north-eastwards then eastwards, passing the Beddingham masts and going forward to a car park at the top end of a road which leads down to the village of Firle. From the road crossing you continue eastwards along the top of the escarpment, but are soon confronted by another climb, albeit fairly gentle, and this brings you to the climax of this walk, Firle Beacon. The trig point is immediately adjacent to the route, again to the left. This is a quite magnificent viewpoint and one of the highlights of the SDW with glorious views in all directions, including a splendid panorama to the north and north-west. Now keeping the fence immediately to your right, continue on the SDW downhill, veering right with the fence and a parallel path now with you to your left. You arrive at a gate which is to your right, and two clumps of gorse immediately to your left. This is your cue to leave the SDW, turning left away from the fence and heading for a signpost with SDW signs pointing right and left and a bridleway heading northwards off the escarpment. Follow this bridleway northwards; it proceeds steeply down the hillside, then on reaching the foot of the hill, you veer to the right, crossing a signed public byway and going forward to reach the buildings of Tilton Farm. Here the path veers sharply left and arrives at a junction with the approach road to Charleston Farmhouse. Turn left to pass (and possibly visit) the farmhouse and cottage garden; for over 60 years this was the retreat of the so-called Bloomsbury Group of artists, writers and intellectuals including Virginia Woolf, Vanessa Bell and David Garnett. It's recently been restored to re-enact the atmosphere of the house as it was in the 1950s, and the shop sells objects inspired by Bloomsbury designs. Beyond the farmhouse the track, proceeding westwards, remains clear but it can be very muddy. You then continue fractionally north of west, through fields; you pass Compton Wood but beyond the wood don't be tempted round to the right, rather kink left into the next field and then continue on clear field paths just north of west, passing the unmistakeable Firle Tower. You pass the bottom end of another wood and reach a junction with a track. Turn right and immediately left downhill through a field then forward along a narrow path between

The Bloomsbury Group's country retreat at Charleston

houses to reach a road at the hamlet of Heighton Street.

Go straight over now onto a signed path through the grounds of Firle Place. The signage is initially good, pointing you across the park, but should you then be unsure I suggest you use as your "rudder" a track to your right, heading just north of west. Aim for a Firle Place sign a little to the left of the junction of that track with the main driveway through the park; on reaching that sign, the continuous route goes straight over, parallel with a path to your right aiming for a gate at the edge of the trees. However you could detour left up the main driveway to visit 16th century Firle Place; its Great Hall has the second largest Van Dyck in the country, and the Long Gallery boasts tremendous views across the park. Whether you've detoured or not, follow parallel with the path towards the gate then veer gently right to reach it, going through it and along a lane which emerges by Firle's shop. Your way is right (north-westwards), past the shop; to visit the village church, turn left onto the road then shortly left again up the path leading directly to the church, returning to the road the same way. Now, whether you've detoured here or not, walk north-westwards along Firle's delightful street, with beautiful flint cottages and a lovely pub, the Ram. Just before the pub, turn right along a signed path, following the sign for the cricket field. Your way is initially on a lane then grass; as you reach the grass, the cricket field to the right, turn left to aim for a gate immediately to the right of the tennis court. Pass through the gate and continue across the field to pass through the gate at the top right corner close to the exit gate for the park. Then walk across the grass to the exit gate as signed, to leave the park, using the side gate if the main gate is shut.

Having exited the park go forward to a road junction; don't turn hard right but go half-right along a road which shortly brings you to the A27. Cross the road with great care and turn left to follow a cycle track parallel with the road, shortly turning right along a narrow road from which there's a great view ahead to Mount Caburn and left to the South Downs. You rise then descend to Glynde's main street, conveniently adjacent to the Trevor Arms pub, turning right here to arrive almost immediately at Glynde station.

Southwick *(Line B, 2 miles, circular walk: easy)*

From the station exit turn right onto the B2167 Station Road and follow it very briefly to reach Albion Street, the main A259 coast road. Cross the road and turn right then immediately before the port authority building, turn left by a sign pointing you to the beach via the lock gates. Follow the walkway then in obedience to the arrow sign, bear right and then veer round to the left to access and cross the

Looking towards Brighton from Shoreham Harbour

lock gates over Shoreham Harbour. Note, however, that the gates frequently open to let harbour traffic through; you may have to wait, but your wait shouldn't be long, and you may enjoy watching the gates part and the boats passing through! Having crossed over it's a short walk to the seafront, where you turn right and follow the concrete promenade round, passing the rocks and simply heading westwards. You veer left onto the harbour wall and continue along it to its very end, the mouth of the Adur; you'll get a superb view to the estuary, Brighton and the cliffs beyond, also Shoreham and its surrounding countryside, and in rough weather you'll be able to enjoy the crash of the waves against the wall.

Retrace your steps all the way to the A259 but this time turn left and very shortly right into Grange Road. Veer left under the railway bridge and go straight onto the green, passing the prominent war memorial and walking round the right-hand edge of it all the way to the top left-hand corner; note the lovely flint cottage on the other side of Victoria Road with a plaque commemorating the painter Douglas Gray. Bear right here into Victoria Road then left into Church Lane to reach the fine church of St Michael, parts of which date back to the 12th and 13th centuries. Walk back down Church Lane, turning left into The Green to reach two splendid houses, the flint-built King Charles Cottage and the flint and timbered Barn. Cross over the green itself to the B2167, turning right and then shortly left into Southwick Square, Southwick's shopping area; while it is quite modern and functional, there's a nice area of gardens at the end on the left. At the T-junction at the end, cross over to look at the attractive Manor Cottage, now a heritage centre and open on Saturdays in summer. Turn left along Southwick Street, walking up to the Methodist Church on the corner of Manor Hall Road; the church is on the site of a Roman villa and there's an information board by the church giving a history of the villa which dates back to around 75 AD, although sadly there is no trace of the villa above the ground. Then retrace your steps down Southwick Street, continuing this time past Manor Cottage and the adjoining Manor, going under the railway and arriving at the station which is on the right.

Stonegate *(Line H, 6 miles, circular walk: moderate)*

Exiting from the station building, turn left onto the station approach road then almost immediately right along a path which heads eastwards up to the buildings of Hammerden. You veer right to arrive at a T-junction of tracks, turning right here, then just past the pond, which is to the right, bear sharp left along a bridlepath. You soon veer right to follow a left-hand field edge, but be careful to veer left after a hundred yards or so, following a not hugely clear path south-eastwards along the right-hand edge of the field, aiming for woodland ahead. Entering the wood, the path becomes clearer; you descend then swing to the right and ascend to arrive at the side of the railway. Veer left and walk briefly parallel with the railway then at a signed footpath junction, cross over the railway, taking great care.

Once over the railway, you are now looking out over the Rother valley. Keep along the signed path, just west of south, but in roughly a hundred yards, with a pond to the right, you need to veer left, south-eastwards across a field, aiming for the bottom end of a line of trees where you should see a footpath signpost, ahead of you. Follow the signed path on along the field edge, veering right to arrive at another footpath signpost which directs you left, across another field. Another signpost reassures you as you continue in the same direction, then shortly reach a path junction at which you turn right, going down to cross the Rother by the curiously named Wreckery Bridge. Continue briefly in the same direction to a path junction. Don't veer away right here with the bridleway but continue southwards along a signed footpath; kink left then immediately right to walk along the right-hand edge of the meadow, keeping Seller's Brook immediately parallel to your right and ignoring a path heading left. Your path continues clearly on southwards, with views to the excellent buildings of Mottynsden to the right. Arriving at a T-junction of footpaths, turn left along the right-hand edge of the pasture, but shortly veer right and follow a clear path which ascends, now within sight of the buildings of Burwash. Another path comes in from the right and "your" path, now a lane, veers left to arrive at Burwash's main street. With its long line of brick-faced houses and shops, many dating back to the 17th and 18th centuries, Burwash is one of the prettiest villages in Sussex; arguably its loveliest house is Rampyndene, built in 1699 and concealing timber-framing beneath its brick façade, on the right-hand side as you head for the church.

Turn left to follow the street past Rampyndene to the junction with School Hill. Cross over School Hill into the churchyard, from the far corner of which there are magnificent views to the countryside to the south, including the obelisk

The pretty village street at Burwash

known as Brightling Needle, the work of an eccentric local MP known as "Mad Jack" Fuller. The church itself boasts a Norman west tower, wide Early English chancel and 14th century iron tomb slab set into a wall at the end of the south aisle, reputed to be one of the oldest of its kind in Sussex. Return to School Hill and now turn left to follow it downhill for roughly half a mile (the road becoming Bell Alley Road); turn right just before a bridge over the river Dudwell along Bateman's Lane, pass the picturesque Old Dudwell Mill and soon arrive at Bateman's. Turn right in front of the house and follow the road briefly to the visitor's entrance to the property which is on your left. Bateman's, now owned by the National Trust, was built in 1634 but gained immortality as the home of Rudyard Kipling between 1902 and his death in 1936. His study has been left just as it was when he was living there; he wrote some of his most popular works here including *Puck Of Pook's Hill* and his poem *If*.

Beyond Bateman's, walk on up the hill for a little under half a mile to arrive at the main road (A265). Turn right to follow it briefly, then turn first left into Spring Lane, descending quite steeply then climbing again to Holton Farm, the road bending noticeably right just before the farm with a bridleway coming in from the left. Very shortly beyond this right bend, the road bends left, and here you bear right onto a signed path, actually a lane heading for Franchise Manor. You soon reach a crossroads of paths where you turn left, north-westwards, shortly climbing some steps then continuing downhill on a narrow but clear path, getting glimpses of the manor complex to your right. You pass the bottom end of a driveway with houses to your right then continue north-westwards to a field corner and straight on across the next field, veering gently left but maintaining a north-westerly course. The way and signage become clearer now as you follow the left-hand edge of fields, and you then veer gently right, following a clear track, and gently left to reach a gate. Go through to arrive at a road, Peartree Hill. Turn right to cross the Rother at Witherenden Bridge and follow the road, passing turnings to the impressive nearby Witherenden Mill and Witherenden Farm. Go forward to cross over the railway, then immediately turn right down the approach road to return to Stonegate station.

Three Bridges *(Line A, 7 miles, linear walk to East Grinstead: moderate)*

Turn right out of the main station exit, walking down to Haslett Avenue East; bear right again to pass under the existing railway, then turn immediately right again to follow Station Hill. Ignore a signed public footpath soon going off to the left, but a little way beyond, just a few hundred yards from Three Bridges station, turn left along a cycleway (signed East Grinstead). You're now on the course of the Three Bridges-East Grinstead railway which opened in 1855 and closed in 1967; it's been converted into a very attractive footpath/cycleway, the Worth Way following its course for much of its length. Follow it briefly now, but after a few hundred yards leave it by bearing right along a signed footpath for Maidenbower, then at the end turn left to follow a path parallel with Maidenbower Drive. You reach a roundabout, using a pedestrian crossing to the left to cross the B2036 and following the roundabout round to its east side. Here you join a signed footpath which initially goes parallel with the B2036 Balcombe Road, keeping on the right side of the fence, then veers eastwards and goes forward to reach Church Road. Turn right then immediately left into Worth Way, soon passing the superb Anglo Saxon church of St Nicholas which is to your right, described by Pevsner as "large in scale and bold in conception." Continue as signed along the Worth Way eastwards, crossing over the M23 then carrying on north-eastwards past Worth Lodge Farm. Just by the farm buildings the Worth Way (your way) veers right, and you follow it to Turners Hill Road; your path veers left to go parallel with this road, then crosses it and continues along the course of the old line.

Rowfant House, just off the popular Worth Way

In less than a mile you arrive at Wallage Lane and the former Rowfant station. The reason the station is here is that the land through which the line passed here was given by an American fur trader and the station was given to him in return. Leave the old line here by turning left into Wallage Lane and following it for a couple of hundred yards to Rowfant Lodge; here turn left as signed onto a driveway, veering right as signed across the grass over a stream to reach another driveway, turning left to reach Rowfant House. Now a restaurant, this is a splendid building originally constructed in the 16th century and although restored in the 19th century retains many Elizabethan features. There's a right of way (Sussex Border Path or SBP) along the driveway through the complex, and it's worth going as far as the attractive stream straight ahead, viewing the rear of the main buildings with attractive tile-hanging. Retrace your steps along the driveway but this time follow it on to Wallage Lane; if there's a problem with exiting the driveway here simply return to Wallage Lane the way you came.

Now proceed briefly eastwards along Wallage Lane, following the course of the SBP (which you'll be on for the rest of this walk) but soon you arrive at a driveway going off to the right, and beyond it a Rowfant Sawmills sign with a footpath sign just next to it. Bear right here onto a narrow signed path which soon brings you back to the Worth Way. Turn left as signed to continue along the Worth Way, almost at once regaining the course of the old line and following it to the B2028 overbridge, the going straightforward and delightful. Shortly beyond this overbridge, you reach a gate but just before it bear right along a path shortly taking you to Grange Road. Turn left to follow it downhill to the sprawling village of Crawley Down.

On reaching the crossroads at the bottom of the hill, turn right along Sandhill Lane, going uphill and then bearing round to the left, eastwards, becoming Burleigh Lane when Sandhill Lane goes off to the right. Continue eastwards along Burleigh Lane to its end, at the buildings of Burleigh House, then join a footpath along the left side of Burleigh House, maintaining your easterly direction and enjoying really lovely views. Continuing eastwards along an obvious path, you gently drop downhill through a succession of fields to cross a stream, then keep going in roughly the same direction uphill, initially through trees then emerging along a clear path through more fields. Look out carefully for the buildings of Tilkhurst Farm which now loom up to your right, just under a mile from Burleigh House, and when you get level with these you reach a footpath junction, turning left and heading just west of north on a clear green path. You soon reach a signpost directing you straight on: do NOT veer right onto the wider track just beyond the signpost but keep going north-westwards on a thinner path, passing the left edge of a pond and going forward to arrive back at the Worth Way. Turn right to follow it for a mile and a half, then when the path ends, bear right round the far end of the upper station car park to your right, going forward across the footbridge over the railway. You arrive in the lower station car park, turning right to arrive at East Grinstead station.

Three Oaks *(Line C, 7 miles, circular walk: moderate)*

(This also covers Doleham - it is recommended that you go straight on to Doleham station; the walk below is described on that basis and 7 miles is the aggregate for both)
Ascend from the platform onto Butcher's Lane, turning right and following it north-eastwards past the pub. In just over quarter of a mile you reach a sign for Half House Farm; don't follow the farm lane but take the path immediately to the left of the lane, heading eastwards away from Butcher's Lane, part of the 1066 Country Walk Hastings Link. The path crosses a field to the edge of woodland (1), then at the corner veers right, south-eastwards, along a left-hand field edge, going forward through woodland and arriving at the A259. Turn right to walk along a pavement beside the road, until you arrive shortly at Church Lane going off to the left. Cross the A259 with care and follow Church Lane, passing the lovely Kennel Cottage with its thatch, weatherboarding and brick, then as directed by the 1066 Country Walk, continue along a path above the lane, keeping it to your right. You go straight on into the churchyard of St Laurence Church, Guestling, a Saxon church with a tower built about 1100. Beyond the church take the 1066-signed path heading to the half-right, south-eastwards downhill, keeping an area of woodland and pond immediately to your right. At the bottom of the hill you cross Lady's Brook to enter Guestling Wood and follow the 1066 walk into the wood; in a couple of hundred yards you reach a path junction where the 1066 walk veers sharply to the right, but you take the path forking left, eastwards. Ignore two paths forking away to the right and reach another path junction where you need to turn left as indicated by the arrow sign, and now head uphill,

Elegant Guestling Church

northwards, through the woods. The woodland is particularly noteworthy for its sweet chestnut trees and, in spring, bluebells and wood anemones, while around Lady's Brook you'll find willow, alder and ash. At the top of the hill you pass a car park and information board, and continue northwards, passing a gap in the woods which is to your right, and arriving at a signed footpath junction. Turn left here and follow the path downhill. Despite crossing tracks your way is obvious until, close to the west edge of the wood, you reach an unsigned path fork; you need to take the right fork here, descending to cross back over Lady's Brook and emerge from the wood. An obvious path now continues westwards, uphill, across a field to a lane, onto which you turn left to arrive back at the church.

If you wished to split the Three Oaks and the Doleham walks you could simply retrace your steps to Three Oaks station from here. However, given the difficulty in accessing Doleham by train, I recommend you now go straight on to Doleham on foot to embark on what is a very fine Doleham station walk. To do this, when you reach point (1) above, don't strike out across the field back to Butcher's Lane but continue along the right-hand field edge path north-westwards to the far corner, following it round and then shortly bearing right to drop down to Butcher's Lane, bearing right along it. Shortly turn left up Fourteen Acre Lane, following it for roughly a mile, then bear left steeply down Doleham Hill to reach the station. Even if you're not alighting from a train here, I recommend you detour to the the tiny station platform, and contrast this with the busier stations you'll have met in Sussex! Then having done so, turn right out of the station along Doleham Lane, dropping to Doleham Ditch, a tributary of the river Brede. You climb a hill, passing a turning to Doleham, and take the first right road turning, enjoying lovely views to the Brede valley. Descend and pass the splendidly converted Little Knight's Oast, shortly bearing right onto the A28 which you now follow across a bridge over the river Brede Bridge and go uphill to Brede village. Having enjoyed the stunning views across the valley from the hilltop, make first for the church of St George, its most interesting feature being the Oxenbridge Chapel and a tomb with effigy of Sir Goddard Oxenbridge, said to have been 7ft tall and popularly known as the Brede Giant. The effigy, completed in 1537, shows his head on a helmet and his feet on a lion! The other feature of note in the church are the modern pictorial depictions of the Stations of the Cross, completed by Thomas Monnington, sometime president of the Royal Academy of Arts, and a modern Madonna carving by the cousin of Winston Churchill. Brede itself is a pretty hilltop village, with a number of attractive cottages including the weatherboarded Church Cottage, the redbrick Marley, a delicious creeper clad cottage on the east side of the main street just by the bus stop and, close by, the handy Red Lion pub.

Retrace your steps to Brede Bridge, then having crossed the bridge bear left onto a riverside path, following the right bank of the river Brede. This is a lovely walk, with beautiful unspoilt meadow surroundings, and wooded hills rising up in the distance. In just under a mile, a little beyond a private footbridge, you reach the Doleham Ditch tributary, and veer right to follow along its right bank, the surroundings still delightful. You reach a footbridge which you cross, switching to the left bank along what is a permissive route taking you back to Doleham Lane. Doleham station is just a short distance away up the hill here to the left, but assuming you're continuing back to Three Oaks station, go straight over the road and continue along the left bank of Doleham Ditch, shortly reaching another footbridge and switching to the right bank, now on the 1066 walk again. You arrive at a gate and 1066 sign and go through the gate as signed to cross over the water, now veering from south-west to south-east and following alongside Sailor's Stream. Go forward to a wide field, walking along a right-hand field edge, arriving at a T-junction at Great Maxfield. Turn left onto a farm lane which shortly veers right, then turn left onto a path, still on the 1066 route, passing through trees and over the railway, going forward to cross two fields. At the end of the second, you reach a fork of paths, where you need to take the right fork, again a 1066-signed path, crossing over two more fields. You rise to reach the end of the second of these fields, and arrive at another path junction; turn hard right here, leaving the 1066 route, and follow an obvious path to arrive at Maxfield Lane. Turn left to reach Butcher's Lane, conveniently just by the Three Oaks pub, and bear right onto Butcher's Lane, shortly reaching Three Oaks station which is to the left.

Uckfield *(Line G, 12 miles, circular walk: strenuous)*

Turn right off the platform into the High Street, crossing the river Uck and following the High Street uphill. Cross the road and turn left into Church Street, some way up the hill, passing the fine part 17th century Old Grammar School and church of Holy Cross, then continue along the street which bends sharp right – you can cut the corner! – then rises and veers left, heading just south of west. You lose the pavement here, so take care. Cross the A22 by a bridge then bear immediately right along a signed path. You soon veer left with the path and drop down through woods, watching for a slight curve to the left where fallen trees can confuse, and cross two footbridges in succession. Emerge from the trees onto a field path which goes forward to meet a track, turning left to follow it gently uphill with a prominent house in view. Pass to the right of the house and go straight on, your path becoming a metalled lane between houses and reaching a T-junction with the Shortbridge road. Go straight over onto a signed but indistinct path through the trees; if in doubt move to the right to follow hard against the fence, but in any event mark your route carefully as you're coming back this way! You arrive at the 12th tee of Piltdown golf course (1) and pass round the back of it to reach the road. Turn right to follow it briefly then turn right onto a signed path which heads north-eastwards to cross part of the picturesque golf course. You soon bear left in obedience to the signpost and now follow the posts in a westerly direction through the rough grass between fairways, passing to the right of a green and then being signed left to return to the road.

Turn right onto the road, soon reaching the lovely Piltdown Pond. There's a waterside path which you can follow parallel with the road, but it goes away from the road with no link path so you'll need to retrace your steps and rejoin the road, continuing to a fork junction. Turn right here to shortly reach a crossroads junction with the busy A272, crossing straight over with care and following the road beyond for a mile, enjoying good views to the left to the Downs, to reach Fletching. This is a lovely village, its highlights being the Norman church of St Mary and St Andrew, the early 18th century Church Farm House immediately to the right of the church, and the castellated gatehouse to Sheffield Park beyond. Just before the gatehouse turn left at the T-junction onto the road signed Newick and follow it for a mile and a half; shortly beyond the pylons you enter an area of trees and houses, and immediately before Forest Lodge turn right onto the signed Ouse Valley Way. Now proceed just west of north through woodland over a crossing track and under pylons, then veer

The entrance to Sheffield Park at Fletching

left to continue north-westwards through meadows beside the Ouse, which is still in its comparative infancy. Following the signposts through the field gates, you arrive at the A275. Immediately opposite is the road leading to Sheffield Park station, the headquarters of the famous preserved Bluebell Railway; even

if you decide not to travel on a train, there's a welcome pub and café!

Whether you've detoured or not, walk briefly north-eastwards up the A275 but almost immediately you'll see on the right the walkers' entrance to Sheffield Park gardens, and you now follow the National Trust-signed path up the hill through the field to arrive at a metalled drive, going straight over to reach the pay kiosk. It's definitely worth visiting the magnificent gardens, laid out by Capability Brown in the 18th century; its 120 acres are renowned for its stunning flowering shrubs in spring and rich colours in autumn. Having visited the gardens, return to the metalled drive and turn right to follow it down to the A275. Turn right to walk beside this busy road to the next crossroads, turning right and following the road, signed Fletching, for just over a mile. Just beyond Splaynes Green Farm turning to the right, you reach a gate into a field (2), and here have a choice. You could continue along the road to Splayne's Green, with its pretty brick cottages and little green and pond, veering right to continue past the imposing Atherall's Farm into Fletching. *Alternatively at (2) you could turn right through the gate and over the field. Pass into another field and turn left to follow the left-hand field edge uphill then through the middle of the next field; go straight on along a very muddy farm track taking you to the road by Atherall's Farm, bearing right onto the road to arrive in Fletching.*

Having reached Fletching, follow the main street past the pub and café/shop, going down to the junction by the church, and turn left. Now retrace your steps all the way back to Piltdown Pond, following the road to point (1) above then make your way past the back of the 12th tee along the indistinct path through the trees – you'll be glad you marked your route so carefully – to to arrive back at the Shortbridge road. Go straight over along the metalled lane, going forward onto the track you followed earlier; don't take the first fork right, but fork next right, a sign on a gate ahead barring further progress straight on! You soon reach the twin footbridges, crossing these then soon veering right, uphill through the trees, swinging sharp right to reach a road just by the bridge over the A22.

Turn left to cross over the A22, then turn left immediately beyond it, through a gate into the Lake Wood area. Take the first path going to the right, and soon climb steps to follow the path keeping the road to your right and a lake and rocky outcrops to your left. It's a lovely piece of walking, a real highlight of your journey back. You swing to the left with your path, drop down again and reach a junction with a wider path onto which you turn right, climbing back to the road and turning left to follow the road back into Uckfield. Bear right at the T-junction at the end and walk downhill past, or possibly into, the many shops and eateries to reach the station at the bottom, noting the smart timber-framed Bridge Cottage by the river crossing.

Wadhurst *(Line H, 8 miles, circular walk: moderate)*

Turn left out of the station, walking through the station car park and bearing left into Station Road, crossing over and almost immediately bearing right into Three Oaks Lane. Veer shortly left with the road, then almost immediately fork left onto a signed path, actually the Sussex Border Path (SBP), which proceeds just east of north then veers just west of north through woodland, on a really excellent wide path. You reach Whitegates Lane and turn left to follow it northwards, veering gently left to the edge of woodland and bearing right, still with the SBP, along a lane leading to Great Shoesmiths Farm. On reaching the farm walk straight through the farm buildings, ignoring paths signed away to the right and left, but follow the signed bridleway heading just east of north along a left-hand field edge with woodland to your left. Beyond the woods you veer very gently to head northwards through pasture, crossing over a footbridge then veering just east of north past a pond and the lovely Bartley Mill to reach Bartley Mill Road. Turn left to follow it briefly, soon forking right along a road uphill through woodland to reach the B2169 Bayham Road.

Turn right to follow Bayham Road for just under a mile through the hamlet of Little Bayham. At length you reach the well-signed turning to Bayham Abbey to your left, and turn left to walk up the approach road, getting excellent views to the Tudor-style (actually 19th century) Bayham Abbey mansion which is to your left. Soon you arrive at the entrance to the ruins of the 13th century Premonstratensian Abbey. Do check the abbey, arguably the most impressive monastic ruin in Sussex, is open before you do the walk! There's a very significant amount still standing, including sections of the nave, cloister, chancel and transepts in a quite glorious setting, and there are beautiful views across the meadows with not only the mansion in sight but a former church (now a private house) in the shade of woodland.

Retrace your steps

Bayham: the most impressive monastic ruin in Sussex?

to Bayham Road, turning left to follow it over Win Bridge. Shortly the road bends left, and immediately beyond this left bend turn right onto a rather inconspicuous path along the edge of trees, soon veering right to follow a left-hand field edge to the field corner. Turn left (eastwards) as signed, then having left the open fields and got within sight of buildings, take care to turn right (this turning could easily be missed) along a path heading most pleasantly south, veering just west of south, through the picturesque little woodland common of Hook Green. You arrive at Free Heath Road, bearing right to follow it uphill to reach a crossroads in the woods. Your way is straight over, but it's worth detouring left for a couple of hundred yards to enjoy a quite superb view northwards across miles of Kent countryside. Then follow the road south of the crossroads to a T-junction with Sleepers Stile Road. Turn left to follow it, soon passing an area of woodland that's to your right, then as you get close to the end of the wood, turn hard right onto a signed path. Ignore forks away to the left, but follow the path as it veers left, southwards, emerging from the wood to cross a field to Newbury Lane. When I walked this section there were alpacas grazing in this field. Turn left into Newbury Lane then shortly right onto a footpath which from its elevated spot (150m) enjoys superb views in all directions, especially to Bewl Water ahead. Follow the path southwards on to Windmill Lane, bearing right onto this road then left at the end and taking the right fork to reach the B2100 at Cousley Wood.

Cross straight over the B2100, passing or patronising the Vine pub which is to your right, and follow Butts Lane southwards, once again on the SBP; veer left with Butts Lane, ignoring the SBP leading off here, and now head very enjoyably downhill just south of east. You arrive at Little Butts Farm, veering sharply right to pass in front of the farm buildings, then just beyond the buildings veer left along a thin path downhill to arrive at the SBP once more. Your way is right here (1), but you should detour left and walk down to the shore of Bewl Water to get beautiful views across the reservoir. Completed in 1975, it's the largest body of inland water in south-east England, particularly popular as a sailing centre and for trout fishing. Now proceed west/south-westwards from point (1), following a really excellent path, popular with walkers and cyclists, through the woods. In a few hundred yards from (1) your path reaches a sharp left bend; ignore the first path leading off your path to the right but having veered southwards, very soon turn right along a second path which heads south-westwards out of the woodland. This very clearly defined path takes you beside trees and then open fields uphill to pass the buildings of Little Pell Farm and arrive at Blacksmith's Lane. Join it and follow it in the same south-westerly direction uphill to arrive in the centre of

Wadhurst, but be warned that the station is still a mile and a half away!

Turn right onto the village street but immediately bear right again into Church Street, then just before the delightful timber-framed and tile-hung Churchgate House bear right into the churchyard. Pass, or possibly detour to visit, the church with its Norman tower and spire which rises to 130ft; go round the far side of the church then turning right to walk round behind it, turning left to enjoy, from the top end of the churchyard, a tremendous view back to Bewl Water. Now follow the obvious path round the left side of the church to return to Church Street, following it to the White House. Turn hard left to walk back down to meet Church Street within sight of the fine Lodge, then right to enter the High Street, and right again up this street. You pass a number of lovely cottages including the Wadhurst Bookshop, and a little way beyond that you reach Wadhurst's finest house, the early 18th century redbrick Old Vicarage, built by John Legas, chief ironmaster of Wadhurst. Keep on along the street uphill, passing junctions with the B2100 going off to the right and shortly Mayfield Lane (B2100 again) going off to the left, in the district known as Durgates. Carry on north-westwards along Station Road, descending to reach the station which is on the left.

Warnham *(Line I, 3 miles, circular walk: easy)*

From the station exit turn right to follow Station Road westwards to the junction with the A24. Cross with immense care and turn left, then bear shortly right along Bell Road to arrive in the centre of the village, noting an excellent weatherboarded house to your left just before the T-junction with the main street. Turn left along Church Street, the Sussex Oak pub to your right and the church of St Margaret to your left; the church is worth exploring with a 16th century chapel and tower, 12th century font, and 1613 monument to Sir John Caryll. Continue along Church Street, passing a parade of shops, then going on past Warnham Court Farm House with attractive tile-hanging. Just before Friday Street on the right-hand side cross over and retrace your steps along Church Street, with several lovely buildings: nos 66 and 64, the timber-framed no 60, the brick-built Warnham Interiors, The Old Cottage, Thorntons, the tile-hung Cokelers, the brown-washed Cobblers, and nos 8 and 6. Just beyond the vicarage turn left along a signed footpath, passing the school and going straight on into Lucas Road. Follow it to a T-junction with Tilletts Lane, turning right to follow it uphill and then turning right into Threestile Road, from which there are excellent views to your left and right.

You continue along the road and begin to descend, passing the splendid timber-framed Old Manor and reaching the village green which is on the right, cutting across the green to reach School Hill. Turn right to follow it to the Bell Road junction, passing several lovely houses which are to your left. These include the redbrick Little Timbers, no 16 with its well, the redbrick Lavender Cottage with 1752 plaque, no 10 with its lovely cottage garden, the adjacent Wallflower Cottage with another immaculate garden, the stone/tilehung Peppercorn Cottage, the unusually named Shatherum, and no 2 on the corner with its imposing brown stone structure. Turn left into Bell Road and retrace your steps to the station via A24 and Station Road.

West St Leonards *(Line H, 2 miles, linear walk to St Leonards Warrior Square: easy)*

Leave the station by the main exit, turning left into St Vincent's Road then right at the T-junction into West Hill Road. Now go first left into Keats Close, crossing the A259 Grosvenor Crescent and going on down Grosvenor Gardens to reach the promenade, turning left to follow it. The promenade is interrupted by the Azur bar complex; simply bear right to follow the lower promenade until you've got beyond the complex. As you get opposite London Road going off to the left, inland from the coast road, leave the promenade and turn left to walk briefly up London Road. Bear left into Norman Road, and immediately to the left you'll see a mural by Ben Eine, a pixelated depiction of Prince Charles. Follow Norman Road to its end then bearing right at the end into Mercatoria and left into Stanhope Place with its lovely multi-coloured houses. At the end turn left into Mews Road, descending and turning left into East Ascent, then as it bends left go straight on along Mount Pleasant before turning right, down the steps, to arrive just east of the Marine Court complex. This is a huge block built in 1937/38 and designed to resemble an ocean liner, and from this angle you can see the resemblance! Bear right to walk to the complex and then walk beside the complex on the coast road side. Beyond the complex turn right into Gardner Way, noting the adjacent gracious Royal Victoria Hotel, then left to pass

Prince Charles at the Love Café

Historic shopfronts at St Leonards

in front of the splendid Assembly Rooms to reach the top of Burton Way. Turn right here; don't carry on up Quarry Hill but bear half-right into St Leonards Gardens, entering by way of South Lodge with its impressive Doric arch. Now walk straight up through the gardens, pausing to enjoy lovely views back to the sea, with very attractive early 19th century houses and villas around the gardens. Many of these are the work of the architect James Burton, who designed the Royal Victoria Hotel and planned to create St Leonards as a Regency seaside resort for the wealthy. Walk uphill, aiming for the north (top) exit at North Lodge, where the author Sir Henry Rider Haggard lived between 1918 and 1923. Exit the gardens by the lodge and continue along Upper Maze Hill; a plaque on Baston Lodge on the right shows that this was the childhood home of Alan Turing, founder of computer science, and whose work was key to breaking the wartime Enigma Code. Continue to the crossroads junction, turning right along Pevensey Road, following it for a few hundred yards then bearing left into Charles Road. Go straight over Dane Road and, shortly beyond Clyde Road on the right, bear right into Gensing Gardens which opened in 1872. Follow a walkway through the gardens initially parallel with Charles Road then veering right to go parallel with Anglesea Terrace, and forking right to go parallel with London Road, effectively therefore going all the way round the gardens. At the end, veer left into London Road and turn right to follow it. Walk past the very impressive church of Christ Church and St Mary Magdalene with its very tall tower, then turn hard left down Kings Road with its multi-coloured buildings and old shop signs, to reach Warrior Square station.

West Worthing *(Line B, 9 miles, linear walk to Worthing: strenuous)*

Walk northwards from the station up South Street, then fork left with South Street and follow it to reach the centre of Tarring village, passing lovely flint cottages and two things of interest: firstly the door to an ancient fig garden (a sign tells you the garden is open one day a year!) and then, in the grounds of a school, the very impressive flint-built Old Palace of the Archbishops of Canterbury, dating back to the 13th century. You reach a crossroads junction (you could detour left here to visit the flint church of St Andrew and also to the right for a better view of the Old Palace) and go straight over into Tarring High Street, a lovely street with beautiful houses, some flint, some brick, some stuccoed, the finest however being the superb 15th century timber-framed Parsonage. Continue up the High Street until shortly before a right bend; opposite no 70, turn left up a narrow alley which soon veers right and brings you to the east end of Pelham Road. Join Pelham Road but then turn immediately right along Stonehurst Road until, just beyond Barton Close which is on the left, you reach another alleyway going off to the right, more or less opposite an alleyway going off to the left. Turn right along this alleyway then cross the A2032, bearing right then immediately left to follow the footpath past a recreation ground to its top end at a junction with Ashacre Lane. Turn left to follow it; it veers to the right, passing Ye John Selden Inn at the junction with Salvington Road, and you go forward northwards up Half Moon Lane to a T-junction with the A27 Crockhurst Hill. Cross this very busy road with great care, and turn left to walk briefly to a sharp left bend, leaving the A27 here to walk northwards (effectively in the same direction) up Mill Lane. Don't fork right onto the signed path but continue uphill on Mill Lane, a rough partially-metalled road which though residential provides good views to Findon Valley and Cissbury Ring beyond. After just over half a mile's non-stop climbing you reach the end of Mill Lane at a crossroads; turn left to immediately reach High Salvington Windmill, a splendid black post mill built in 1750, open two Sundays a month in summer. Then from the crossroads carry on along Bost Hill, emerging from the woods to enjoy further excellent views towards Cissbury Ring.

Continue downhill, veering right to reach the

The old Archbishops' Palace at Tarring

Bost Hill car park which is to your left, and noting the attractive open space, the Gallops, to your right. Just beyond the car park bear left onto a signed bridleway and follow this narrow and well-defined path north-westwards. You go over a signed path crossroads, very shortly bearing left to reach the buildings of Roger's Farm; follow the path to the end, amongst the buildings, and turn right to head northwards along the farm lane. At the sharp left bend, ignore the right fork and bear left to pass a lodge, then shortly turn right onto a signed footpath which follows the lower slopes of South Park, heading northwards to reach a junction with a lane in the shade of trees. Turn left and walk up the lane, part of the Monarch's Way long-distance footpath, to pass the superb 18th century Findon Place and arrive at the lovely flint-built church of St John the Baptist in an idyllic setting, again in the shade of trees below Church Hill. Its original structure dates back to the 11th or 12th century and the church contains a rare 13th century oak screen and medieval oak pews. Retrace your steps down the lane and this time go forward to cross the busy A24 dual carriageway, then immediately beyond the crossing bear left onto a signed but rather slippery footpath north-eastwards through a field. You arrive at High Street by Findon Manor, turning left to follow High Street to the crossroads in the centre of Findon village which with its pretty flint cottages and sturdy stone buildings, some dating back to the 16th century, boasts a remarkable range of pubs, shops and eateries.

Turn right along Nepcote Lane, following it south-eastwards through the village, gently uphill. Immediately beyond a sharp right bend, in just over quarter of a mile, turn left up the road signed for Cissbury Ring, and follow it eastwards uphill. The road ends at a car park immediately below Cissbury Ring; just by the car park you descend a few feet then turn right to arrive at a signed crossroads of paths. You need to take the path heading straight on, aiming for a gate at the foot of the steep hill, going through the gate and carrying on uphill, going forward to climb steps as the gradient intensifies. You go straight over the outer ring and continue up the steps to reach the inner ring (1). Go straight over again, onto a green path which takes you unerringly to the trig point at the summit of the Iron Age hillfort of Cissbury Ring. The views are astonishing, perhaps the most rewarding ones being eastwards towards Brighton and beyond, and westwards across a massive stretch of coast as far as the Isle of Wight.

Retrace your steps to (1) and now turn left to follow the inner ring southwards, enjoying fabulous views to the west. Shortly before the inner ring veers to the left, bear right down a set of steps to reach the outer ring, and turn left to follow the outer ring, veering left, eastwards, the hillside now dotted with trees. You pass a stile and continue to a gate immediately before a patch of thicker woodland; turn right here through the gate and follow a path downhill, keeping the woodland to your left. Soon you reach a crossroads of paths, and here go straight over along a good path in a southerly direction. Initially you maintain height and enjoy good views, but then as you pass a golf course, you begin to lose height and it's then a steady descent, through woodland to drop down to the A24. Cross over carefully and turn left to walk beside the A24 on the far side, passing to the right of the roundabout and remaining beside the A24, Broadwater Street West. Soon you reach an attractive green immediately to the right; walk through the gap in the fencing to follow its left side, then at the far end turn left onto Ardsheal Road immediately arriving at the A24 again. Cross it and follow its left side to enter Broadwater village, passing a modern parade of shops including an inviting café. Bear left into Broadwater Street East, noting two lovely red-brick cottages on the left a short way down the street, then turn right into the churchyard and follow it round to the right to reach the main church entrance. The church dates back to the 12th century and is extremely attractive with one particularly memorable 15th century brass of John Mapilton. Walk straight from the main entrance to the A24, turning left to follow it briefly to a crossroads junction of the B2223 and Carnegie Avenue. Turn right to follow the latter, soon reaching the Broadwater & Worthing cemetery which is to your right; guided tours of the cemetery are available at certain times as there are many very notable burials and memorials. At the crossroads turn left into South Farm Road, and follow it, passing a good supply of shops and the odd café which are on the right. At length you reach a level crossing; go over it and immediately beyond the crossing turn left into Cross Street to arrive at Worthing central railway station.

Winchelsea *(Line C, 6 miles, linear walk to Rye: moderate)*

From the station platform walk down to Station Road and turn right to follow it for half a mile or so to meet the A259 on a very sharp bend. Turn right up the A259, Ferry Hill, and then bear first left under the splendid Pipewell Gate, one of three surviving medieval town gates, to enter the centre of the present Winchelsea village. Following a storm in 1287 which washed most of the old town away, a new town was built, its grid pattern making it effectively England's first piece of town planning, and the grid pattern can still be seen today, with well spaced out houses, some of which are weatherboarded or tile-hung and/or decorated with climbing roses and wisteria. Continue up North Street then bear first right into Hiham Green and follow it to a crossroads junction (1) with the High Street, noting the splendid New Inn on the corner. Turn right and follow the

High Street to its junction with the A259, from which there is a great view across the valley of the Brede; cross and turn left to note the ruins of Blackfriars then cross back to look at the late 18th century Wesley chapel. Retrace your steps to the junction at (1) above, turn right (crossing to visit the Wesley Tree, site of where John Wesley preached an open air sermon) and follow this road, initially German Street then Monks Walk, leaving the town. As this road veers round to the right, carry straight on along a narrow road, looking back to your left to enjoy splendid views to Greyfriars, a house built immediately beside the site of an early 14th century Franciscan church (the ruins are still there but not open to the public). Continue down the narrow road, which has a delightful rural feel, to arrive at New Gate, the second of the three medieval gateways into the town, the setting of this one remote and apparently quite incongruous! Beside it is a fragment of the town ditch and looking westwards here there's an excellent view to the lovely Wickham Manor. Retrace your steps up the road, until it veers right, and here you join a signed footpath heading northwards keeping a fence to the right. You soon reach a footpath junction and here fork right, aiming for an impressive stone ruin ahead; it's actually a section of the old St John's Hospital. You reach the road, turning right and veering left, back up Monks Walk. As you arrive at a crossroads with the church to your half right, turn right into Back Lane and follow it to its end, bearing left into Rookery Lane, a lovely part of the town with beautiful views. Then at the crossroads turn left into the High Street and at the next crossroads, left again into St Thomas Street. At the end turn hard right into the churchyard and walk to the church with its marbled effigies and canopies and pinnacled tombs that are some 700 years old. Then continue across the churchyard to the 18th century New Inn, joining the High Street here and following it eastwards, passing the Court Hall, believed to date back to the first days of the "new" town and now containing a museum. You should detour second left into Castle Street to view the Town Well (and the preserved notice from the town's magistrates!) and adjacent Armoury, a splendid stone building of 14th century origin; you should also detour down Barrack Square to view the fine tile-hung Old Cambric Factory. Keep on along the High Street past a shop and café, reaching a sharp left bend with a lovely view towards the sea (Tower Cottage to the right here was the sometime home of actress Ellen Terry), and passing under or round the side of the third medieval gate, Strand Gate. Drop down to reach the A259 again and turn right to follow it.

As the road bends left, bear right into Sea Road, following this road just south of east for a little over half a mile until it swings sharply right. Leave the road here by following a lane eastwards, the same direction as the road had been following, soon swinging left (northwards) and then veering right (eastwards) again, passing Castle Farm which is to the right. The lane forks and you bear left, following an obvious track through the grass towards the spectacular ruin of Camber Castle. As you approach the castle you go through a gate, just beyond which you reach a fork of paths (2); your way forward is straight on along the main path, keeping the fence to your left, but you need to fork right here to detour to the castle, and then turn right again as you get level with the castle to arrive at the entrance. The castle was constructed in 1539 on orders from Henry VIII, and at its peak of activity in 1542 it had a garrison of 42 men, but the main fortifications were demolished a century later. Return to (2) and now follow the main path which continues north-westwards with the fence to the

Strand Gate, one of Winchelsea's three old town gates

left, enjoying good views towards Rye and across the Brede valley. A few hundred yards beyond the castle you reach a gate and a bridge over a channel. Pass through the gate and cross the bridge, bearing right to follow an obvious embankment path with the channel to the right and the river Brede close by to your left. Keep on the embankment, veering right as signed at a gate, then veer gently left, going forward along a wide stony track which takes you to the Rye Harbour road. Turn left along it, shortly turning right onto the main A259 which brings you into Rye. Just before a bridge crossing of the river Tillingham you can detour left along a signed path taking you to a railway crossing, immediately before which there's an excellent view of Rye's windmill, then return to the A259; whether you've detoured or not, cross the Tillingham and immediately reach a mini-roundabout. Go straight over along Wish Street, keeping the café to your left and inn to your right and reaching a junction with a road going to the left, Ferry Road; turn left along this road, shortly veering round to the right with Station Approach and soon reaching the station which is to your left. Of course you may wish to go on immediately to undertake the Rye station walk!

Wivelsfield *(Line E, 6 miles, linear walk to Haywards Heath: moderate)*

From the station, walk down to Leylands Road and follow it briefly eastwards past shops and cafes, then at the junction turn left and follow Valebridge Road northwards. In just over a quarter of a mile, just after the houses recede to the left, turn left onto a signed footpath. You shortly cross the railway then turn immediately right onto a path that runs parallel with the railway then veers a little left, away from the embankment, now in the Bedelands Nature Reserve. You pass through a small area of woodland then on emerging take a left path fork through the pasture and aim for a signpost at the edge of the trees. Follow the path as signed, passing to the left of a lovely pond, and over a bridge, noting a picturesque waterfall just below the bridge to the left which feeds off the pond waters. Continue northwards under a line of pylons to reach a T-junction of paths, turning right. You shortly reach a lane going off to the left; turn left and follow it uphill past Brooklands Farm, with excellent views to the South Downs escarpment behind. In a little over a quarter of a mile you enter a wooded area and turn left as signed to enjoy a very pleasant walk along the edge of woodland with pasture to your right, heading north-westwards and descending gently. Just below Little Burchetts you veer left and walk westwards to reach the A273.

Turn right to walk alongside this road for just under half a mile; fortunately there are verges so you won't need to dodge the traffic. At some stage you need to cross over, negotiating a left bend in the shade of trees, then veer right, with the luxury of a pavement on your side of the road. Shortly beyond this right bend, just beyond a rather imposing gated entrance and driveway beyond, turn left onto a signed path through a field, veering right at the path fork and entering an attractive area of woodland. Follow the clear path downhill through the wood, then emerge and proceed gently uphill through pasture, aiming between a further patch of woodland to the left, and a lovely redbrick house to the right. Pass immediately to the left of the garden of the house and continue on to a crossing track, going straight over and following a very narrow path, crossing the A272 and following another very narrow path to a T-junction of paths, turning left. Initially it's narrow going through the trees, but then you emerge and follow an obvious course through fields, enjoying super views to the Downs. You pass a small area of woodland noting Newbury Pond to your right; your path becomes Newbury Lane, gaining height, and you can see the spire of Cuckfield church to your right. As you get pretty much level with the church (and just before another track goes off to the left), turn right to walk through the cemetery, using a path to walk towards the church then left to aim for the chapel of rest. Pass just to the right of it and arrive back at Newbury Lane, turning right to follow it to a junction with the B2036 on the edge of Cuckfield.

Turn left to follow the B2036 south-westwards past the driveway to the house known as Cuckfield Park, going on to the cricket ground and

The charming houses by the churchyard in Cuckfield

turning right to walk past the cricket pitch to get an excellent view of Cuckfield Park itself, Elizabethan in origin. Now retrace your steps up the B2036 and follow it into the centre of Cuckfield, a delightful little town with many pretty cottages and houses. Its highlights are the splendid 16th century timber-framed Ockenden Manor, now a hotel, up Ockenden Lane off the main street to the left, Church Street with its lovely timbered Nonsuch House on the left, the churchyard and pretty brick cottages on its fringe which provide more splendid downland views, and the part 13th century church of the Holy Trinity with its towering spire which was completed in the 14th century. The sturdy stone Kings Mews, on the corner of Church Street and the main street, is also most impressive. Returning to the main street and following it uphill, you'll reach the town museum, the highlight of which is its display on the Cuckfield Dinosaurs and the work of a local palaeontologist who reputedly discovered the first fossilised iguanodon teeth!

From the museum walk back down the hill, cross the main street and turn left to follow Broad Street eastwards away from the centre. The road bends gently right just beyond the B2184 London Lane coming in from the right; you pass Horsgate Lane then as Broad Street bends slightly right again turn left into Hatchgate Lane. As the lane bends left to become Wheatsheaf Lane, fork right along a footpath which proceeds pleasantly through the Blunts Wood nature reserve, a haven for wildlife which may include stoats, weasels and voles. You emerge at Blunts Wood Crescent, walking along it to Blunts Wood Road, onto which you turn left. Now follow it, going straight on along Harlands Road; you reach a fork junction and need to take the left fork, Bannister Way, passing Sainsbury's and going straight on under the railway bridge. Haywards Heath station is immediately beyond the bridge on the right.

Worthing *(Line B, 2.5 miles, circular walk: easy)*

Go southwards from the main station exit to the traffic light junction with Teville Road. Cross the road and turn left to follow Teville Road briefly, then right into Christchurch Road, following it past the law courts to its junction with Richmond Road. Turn left then shortly right into Portland Road. You soon pass the magnificent flint-built Christ Church which is to your right; immediately opposite is Ambrose Place, well worth detouring along, with beautifully kept private gardens to your right, and a fine row of balconied houses to the left. There's a plaque on the wall of no 14 showing that the playwright Harold Pinter lived here between 1962 and 1964. Continue on down Portland Road, noting further lovely flint-built houses at nos 98, 100 and 102, then at the crossroads bear left into Shelley Road. Shortly turn right into Liverpool Terrace, arguably Worthing's most elegant street, designed and built in the early 19th century, with its impressive line of bow fronts. Walk on to cross Montague Street, and pass along Montague Place

The Dome, built in 1910; Worthing's most distinctive seafront building

to arrive at the seafront; cross the coast road, Marine Parade, and turn left to follow the promenade, soon reaching and perhaps detouring along the pier. This dates from 1862 but has suffered badly over the years from extremes of weather and also fire.

You continue along the promenade, passing Worthing's most photogenic building, The Dome, which dates back to 1910, and the fine Steyne Gardens, both over the coast road to your left. A little further, also to the left on Beach Parade, is a fine parade of white-painted residences and apartments, while the popular beach attraction Splash Point, with its sculpted rocks, is to the right. Beyond the popular Aquarena complex which is to the left, the promenade veers decisively to the left then right again, running parallel with New Parade; at the far end of New Parade look out for the Esplanade going away to the left. On the redbrick block on the far side of the Esplanade is a blue plaque to Oscar Wilde who wrote *The Importance Of Being Earnest* in a house on this site in 1894, and named one of the play's leading characters after the town. Now retrace your steps to Steyne Gardens and this time cross the coast road to enjoy the gardens, and their focal point, the magnificent Boer War memorial. Keeping the very fine Chatsworth Hotel just over the road to the left, follow the path up the west side of the gardens inland (northwards) parallel with and then veering left into the Steyne, a magnificent four-storeyed terrace with grey upper storeys and white lower ones. At the top end of the Steyne, bear left into Warwick Street, following it westwards – it's worth detouring along the early 19th century Bedford Row which is to your left – to reach Chapel Road. On the right corner of Warwick Street and Chapel Road, known as South Place, is a bank which was once the Town Hall, built in Grecian style in 1834. Turn right up Chapel Road to reach a trio of really imposing buildings on the left, interrupted by Richmond Road. First, on the south side of Richmond Road, is the 1812 St Paul's Church with its four-column Greek Doric portico, then on the far side of Richmond Road is the impressive red brick art gallery and museum, particularly noteworthy for its early 19th century paintings, with especially fine Victorian watercolours; the museum's costume and toy collections are amongst the largest in the country and there's an exciting programme of contemporary and historical exhibitions. Immediately beyond the museum is the neo-Georgian Town Hall, opened in 1933 by Prince George, later the Duke of Kent, and containing beautiful pastel coloured mosaics with maritime themes. On the other side of Chapel Road, just before the Post Office, is Union Place, which contains the very distinctive Connaught Theatre. Having detoured to visit the Town Hall, head westwards along Richmond Road, turning right into Christchurch Road and retracing your steps to the station.

*

So concludes our exploration of East and West Sussex via walks around their railway stations. S B Publications has numerous books which explore many of these places and their fascinating histories in further detail. See overleaf for more information.

Looking towards Highdown Hill (Goring-by-Sea, page 81)

S B Publications

S B Publications has numerous titles which cover in further detail many of the areas and places touched on in these pages. Information on these can be found at:

www.sbpublications.co.uk

Layout by Vital Signs Publishing
Email: *info@vitalsignspublishing.co.uk*